The Elders

of

the Church

LAWRENCE R. EYRES

PRESBYTERIAN AND REFORMED PUBLISHING CO.
Phillipsburg, New Jersey

ISBN: 0-87552-258-0

TABLE OF CONTENTS

and para-ecclesiastical organizations are at full noon. Old lines are being erased; new ones are being drawn. Churches and organizations, once inimical to Calvinistic thought and presbyterian church government, seem not only willing but (in many cases) anxious to reexamine their own beliefs and practices in the light of the Reformed interpretation of the Scriptures. But the question is, as they begin to take a closer look, what will they see? A vigorous faith riding triumphantly in a sturdy chariot or a would-be victor limping along beside an all but disabled conveyance?

We who espouse presbyterianism as the nearest expression of biblical truth, dare not miss the opportunities of the hour—we dare do nothing less than repair the Church where she has broken down, refashion her where she was never wholly true to the Designer's plans, and provide a fit vehicle for His truth. Some of us have been working hard to heal the wounds in homes and among members of the Church by a new emphasis upon biblical counseling, pastoral work and care and discipline. But the next step is to mount a new and virile effort to strengthen the very fabric of the Church herself. That is why Lawrence Eyres, pastor of the Orthodox Presbyterian Church of Dayton, Ohio is to be commended for this timely, practical effort to clarify and expound the biblical principles of Church polity in a fresh way. Presbyterian doctrine and presbyterian polity go hand-in-hand. The former depends more upon the latter for its proper demonstration than many realize. We shall miss our opportunity, therefore, if we pay little heed to the subject of church government. Church government—do the very words sound dull and lifeless to you? When you hear those words do you think only of routines and reports? Of parliamentary procedure and committees? Well, if so, you do not conceive of the subject as you should. The Church is *His* Church over which our Lord, Jesus Christ, reigns as Head and King. It

PREFACE

The publication of a study on Church government is no ordinary event; it never was, but that is especially true today. "Why get excited over a study of church government" you ask. I'll tell you why. Because whether our churches recognize it or not, one of the greatest needs and greatest challenges that lies before the present generation of Christians is the construction of a new virile church to enter into what could be the greatest opportunity to serve Jesus Christ that has been known on this Continent. Unless I am greatly mistaken, the opportunity lies immediatedly ahead; but it will not be bought up unless there is a sound organization devised and built along strictly biblical lines, functioning to the glory of God and the building of strong churches and strong Christians. Otherwise all of the efforts, all of the gains, all of the victories will amount to little more than a flash in the pan; nothing solid, nothing lasting will be conserved.

Today, as never before, biblical Christianity is reemerging tall from the smoking ruins of a once-proud but shattered liberalism. Liberals everywhere are on the retreat. The nation is perplexed by moral, political and economic confusion and chaos. Neither science nor psychology has been able to stem the tide. Jaded by it all, many are looking for a place to turn for help. A new interest in the biblical faith of John Calvin and Martin Luther is seen among young people. Conservative seminaries flourish,

v

is through that Church that He is redeeming lost sinners and building up believers to render service to the honor of His Name. It is this Church that He gifted with officers to organize and to lead her in the paths of righteousness for His Name's sake. It is the members of this same Church that on every continent lift their hands in prayer and their voices in praise to His Name as King of Kings and Lord of Lords! In a peculiar way He has tied His name to His Church. The study of Church government, therefore, involves the study of how to exalt the Name of Christ. No, the study of Church government need not be dull; indeed it *is* not dull, and we dare not *make* it so. For the study of Church government is nothing less than the study of the ordinary ways and means by which Jesus Christ is now at work in this world glorifying Himself. He is in the midst of the lampstands. Let us study then, that we may know how best to fashion each lamp so that its light may burn most brightly.

Mr. Eyres' study grows out of a mature exposure to the problems of biblical Church government. He is at once theoretical, and practical. By exegetical work, he endeavors not only to uncover biblical principles, but from them also draws implications and makes applications in useful workaday terms. These studies first appeared serially in the *Presbyterian Guardian*, and are now released with the intention of stirring new interest in the subject of governing Christ's Church. They will provide grist for a number of fruitful discussions among the members of any board of elders. Pastor Eyres, we the members of the Church of Jesus Christ owe you a debt of gratitude. Thank you for making these materials available!

Jay Adams, 1974
Westminster
Theological Seminary
Philadelphia, Penna.

INTRODUCTION

Of all the honors given to sinful men, none exceeds that of being impressed into the life-long service of the King and Head of the church. Though Paul called himself the chief of sinners, he also magnified his office. Well he might, for the risen Lord laid on him that high calling when he confronted Saul of Tarsus on the Damascus road.

That was a sovereign call—no negotiations, no drawing up of terms, no waiting a reasonable time for Saul's consent. Saul *was* willing because the Lord *made* him willing "in the day of his power."

It was also a unified call—not first to discipleship (to just "being saved") and then to apostleship (to a specialized life of service). It was all one thing. When Jesus called Paul, it was to bondservice to the Lord *and* into apostleship to the Gentiles *all in one.*

What has the call of Saul to do with "The Elders of the Church?" Peter, an apostle speaking to elders, described himself as one "who am also an elder." Peter was not an apostle *and* an elder. Rather, the special office of the apostle contained within it the more general office of elder. The apostles were elders extraordinary. Acknowledging this as a general principle, it follows that the principles inherent in the call to apostleship are also inherent in the call to eldership, the only earthly rule now in the church. Therefore, if the apostolic calling may not be viewed as two but as a unified calling to faith *and* to apostleship, so the call to the eldership is not two but one.

Some will object, saying that the call to faith in Christ must come years prior to the call to rule in the church, and that there are really two distinct callings. I would answer that, if the Holy Ghost makes men bishops (elders),

1

then the calling to the latter is but a delayed aspect of a man's initial calling to faith in Christ. Every call to faith is also and always a call to service. Or to repeat a saying I heard some years ago, *The man who is called to preach the gospel, if he follows any other calling, is a lost soul.*

Underlying assumptions

It is time now to tell you where we shall be going in these articles. Before I do, I want to disclaim any attempt to be comprehensive or profound. Nor do I mean to contend for or against the "two-office" or "three-office" views current in Presbyterian circles. My own conviction is that the two-office position is the more biblical one, that there are only two permanently ordained offices in the church, that of elder and of deacon. Years of study and of wrestling with the biblical data convince me that there is no essential distinction between the office and function noted in Scripture under the titles of bishop, elder, pastor, or rule and governments. There are distinctions of labor within that office, but the office of elder is itself but one.

Another assumption I want to lay down as fundamental is that the individual church or local congregation is scripturally ruled by a plurality of elders. This seems clear from many New Testament references; James 5:14 and Acts 14:23 eloquently support this assumption. It follows that the only legitimate one-man rule in the church is that of the one Man whom Peter calls "the chief Shepherd."

My final unargued assumption is that the office of the elder (and normally, its exercise also) is for life and may not be laid down except for good and necessary reasons. Some men, upon being elected to the eldership for a term of years, will justify their acceptance of office on the ground that every man must be ready to serve his turn. This is no different from the attitude of the young man who feels he ought to serve his stint in his country's armed forces, though he has no interest in a military career. Can you imagine Peter or Paul talking this way, of being ready to leave their nets or tentmaking to "take their turn" at "apostling" for a three- or six-year hitch?

These assumptions are made without further argumentation so that we may devote more attention to developing the following propositions. The substance of the remaining articles of this series is either contained or implicit in these

2

six propositions:

1. Elders are made by the Holy Spirit of Christ.

2. Adult (confessing) Christians are endowed with the spiritual capacity to discern those whom the Holy Spirit has made elders.

3. Elders, in the fulfillment of their holy calling, hold the key to the health of the congregations under their rule.

4. Biblical submission to elders cannot be expected except where the congregation has exercised its choice as to who its elders should be.

5. No man can safely be ordained to the office of elder who does not possess *all* the biblically stated qualifications for that office.

6. The elders of the church are co-pastors, and every use of the office should reflect this fact.

I want to conclude this first article with a personal word. I have been an elder in Christ's church long enough not to need Paul's counsel to Timothy, "Let no man despise thy youth." But it is not that I "know" so much about the eldership after all these years. Many know far more than I.

My only reason for undertaking to write on this subject is that something needs to be said. Witness the recurring tragic upheavals in churches. To borrow the language of James, "My brethren, these things ought not so to be." The cure of these "diseases" in our churches must come from those men whom the ascended Lord has equipped for his church, the elders. I earnestly pray that these articles may in some small way point to a beginning of the healing (and that not "slightly"!) of "the hurt of the daughter of my people."

1

MADE BY GOD, NOT BY MEN

As we said last time, if a congregation seeks to be governed biblically, it must be ruled by a plurality of elders. The evidence from Scripture is overwhelming; one-man rule in the church is not what Scripture teaches.

Even so, some Christians including Reformed ones have failed to see this clearly. The reason seems to be that, though they may have a plurality of elders, they view the pastor as having a distinct and unique office. And in effect, they tend to allow him to rule alone.

The Bible does not permit this distinction. It does enunciate (in 1 Timothy 5:17) a difference between those "who rule well" (i.e., elders) and those (also elders) who not only rule well but also "labor in the word and doctrine." The difference is not between two offices, with pastor distinguished from elders, but a difference of function *within* the one office of elder. Of the whole body of those who rule well (all elders), there are some (pastors) who give themselves wholly to the Word and to teaching.

All of these elders are "worthy of double honor" worthy of financial support by the congregation to the extent needed for the labors of their office. It is the pastors, whose time is wholly given to their office, who particularly need such support (cf. verse 18). But all of these, the pastor and other elders, are included within those "who rule well." All of these, as elders, are included within the office whose qualifications are set forth in such places as 1 Timothy 3:1-7 and Titus 1:7-9. These instructions apply to *all* who are rightfully called elders, whether they are what we call ruling elders, or whether they are pastors, missionaries, or teachers.

"The Spirit has made you bishops"

Our proposition, in the title above, is that all elders worthy of the name are made elders by God, and not by men. (In succeeding articles I shall deal with the question as to how the church is to recognize and set apart those men, and only those, whom God has made elders.)

How can I be so positive about this? We should first look at Acts 20:28, in which Paul says, "The Holy Ghost hath made you overseers." Three facts need to be kept in mind here: (1) These words are part of Paul's farewell address *to the elders* of the church at Ephesus, and are all the more gravely made since Paul expects never to see these men again in the flesh. (2) The word translated "overseers" in the King James' Version is more usually and correctly translated "bishop" (as in 1 Timothy 3 and Titus 1). (3) In Paul's writings, the terms "bishop" and "elder" are used interchangeably (cf. Acts 20:17 and verse 28 itself).

In other words, we are warranted in understanding that it is the elders themselves about whom Paul is speaking in verse 28. A free paraphrase of the verse might read: "Look well to your own lives and conduct, and also to the life of the whole church, considered as Christ's flock, over which the Holy Spirit has established you as elders, to fulfill the role of shepherds to God's blood-bought people." Notice that Paul says that the Holy Spirit *made—established, constituted*—these men elders in Christ's church.

Christ has given gifts to men

Again, Paul writes in Ephesians 4:7-11 what is no less to the point here. To summarize, the Apostle says that the Lord Jesus has measured out gifts to his church. These gifts he purchased, or merited, by means of his atoning death upon the cross, by which he also destroyed the Devil's power over the church. And he broke the power of death over his people by his death and resurrection.

Having completed what he came to earth to do, Christ ascended to heaven and then poured out gifts upon his church. We need to distinguish between *the gift* that the risen Lord gave his church, and the many and varied *gifts* he gives to men for his church. The gift, as Peter tells us in Acts 2:23, is none other than the Spirit who first came to the church at Pentecost. But this gift of the Spirit under-

5

lies Paul's discussion of gifts in Ephesians 4, as well as in 1 Corinthians 12:6-11 where it is such "charismatic" gifts as prophecy, tongues, and healing that Paul is discussing.

In Ephesians 4:11, Paul is speaking of gifted *men*: "And he gave some, apostles; and some, prophets; and some, evangelists; and some, pastors and teachers." The evangelists and teacher-pastors are perpetually given by Christ to his church on earth as his full supplying of the church's needs, flowing forth from his complete victory over Satan, sin and death. As the outworking of the given Spirit, the Lord gives men gifts and thus sovereignly qualifies them as gifts to the church for the perfecting of the saints. These men of gifts and only these are to be the elders of the church.

So also Peter exhorts the elders among those to whom he wrote (in 1 Peter 5:1-4). Peter says of himself that he is "also an elder." On what basis can he claim this? Nowhere do we read that, subsequent to Peter's being called as an apostle, he was ever chosen as an elder in addition.

Peter's eldership must be understood as being encompassed in his calling to be an apostle, a calling received from the Lord Jesus. In other words, we may say that *all apostles were elders*—though it does not follow that all elders were apostles by any means. The apostles were simply elders extraordinary. From which we may conclude that Peter, being made an apostle by the Lord, was also made an elder by the Lord. And so must it be for those who are elders in Christ's church ever since. Christ gave apostles to the church; and Christ continues to give elders, men of gifts, to the church.

When Paul warns Timothy to "lay hands (in ordination) suddenly on no man," he is implying the same truth (in 1 Timothy 5:22). Paul had already (in 3:1-7) laid down a careful summary of the gifts required: an advanced level of sanctification, ability to teach, ability to rule, some fourteen qualifications in all. These are *required* of all elders. They are gifts of God, not man-made. And sufficient time should be allowed for such gifts to show themselves before a man is given the high office of elder. Such a man was Timothy himself whom Paul calls a "man of God" (1 Timothy 6:11).

6

God makes elders — implications

It may fairly be concluded, therefore, that these passages teach us that *God alone makes elders.* God makes men elders, and the church's duty is to discern which men God has given to the church for teaching and ruling.

This truth must be stressed; it is not incidental. Everything that follows in this series can be traced from this basic truth about elders. There are, however, three important implications to mention now:

(1) Great care must be exercised when choosing elders. In part this is true because the signs of qualification for the office are often misread even when care is exercised. Human evaluation of subjective personal qualities is fallible at best. As Paul told the Ephesian elders, men ordained under his ministry, "Also of your own selves shall men arise, speaking perverse things, to draw away disciples after them" (Acts 20:30).

If that is the case, we might be driven to say, "What's the use? You can't be sure of anyone, so why try?" No, ours should be the opposite reaction, the reaction of Paul himself who says simply, "Therefore watch!" Secret hypocrisy is to be found in the church; but that is no reason for us to grant open hypocrites and weaklings the crucial office of the elder.

(2) If God makes men elders, it becomes rather dangerous for any congregation to determine in advance how many elders it will have. This danger is frequently present in home missions work when a new group of believers is eager to become a full-fledged church. They look over the men and ask, "Which of these should we make elders?" Too often the presbytery simply goes along.

When an arbitrary number is the main criterion for choosing men to be elders, the church will certainly pay for its folly when such men turn out to be scripturally unqualified. And there is often no end to the payments! A new congregation where true "men of God" are not clearly distinguishable ought to postpone the date for its full organization until God sends it his own manifest choices. One thing we can be certain about is that God *will* send such men in due time. The Lord of the church is not remiss in distributing the needed gifts to his elect people!

(3) Finally, if God makes men elders, it is equally as unwarranted to pass by the obviously God-made man as it is to give unqualified men this high office. In larger and outwardly more prosperous churches this can be a real danger. We begin to pass by those men who lack educational polish or financial position or social prestige, in effect making these into qualifications for the office. But if God has evidently laid his hand on the uneducated man, the social nobody of limited income, let the church be sure to lay hands of ordination on such a man of God. To do otherwise is to give affront to the Head of the church!

The Lord Jesus Christ is the sovereign Head of the church, working through the Holy Spirit whom he sent and gave to the church. But the Spirit's working is not capricious. The congregation of Jesus Christ that waits—and waits with earnest prayer—upon its Lord will not be abandoned by him to the weakness and caprice of men. God will send his own men, those whom he has enabled to give of themselves to promote the purity, peace and true unity of his church.

Psalm 133:2 presents us with a beautiful picture of the Lord's intention for his people. Peace and unity among the brethren is a benediction from heaven itself. As the anointing oil was poured over the head of the high priest Aaron, and as its fragrance ran down his beard to the very skirts of his robe, so the commanded blessing comes upon Zion. The blessedness of peace and unity comes down from the Head of the church to give fragrance to the whole church which is his body. And the primary human instruments, by his Word and Spirit, who serve as the means through which the blessing comes upon us from our Lord, are those men given by Christ—the elders of the church. God give us such men that we might be blessed through their labors!

8

2

SELECTED BY THE CHURCH

"Though the character, qualifications and authority of church officers are laid down in the Holy Scriptures, as well as the proper method of their investiture and institution [i.e., ordination and installation], *yet the election of the persons to the exercise of this authority, in any particular society, is in that society."*

This statement is in the chapter on "Preliminary Principles" of biblical church government in the *Form of Government* of the Orthodox Presbyterian Church. Simply put, we are told that, though the rulers of the church must be chosen with due regard for the biblical requirements of their office, it is still the church itself that must do the choosing and not some outside body.

In the previous article I sought to show from Scripture that it is God who makes men elders (including those we call ministers). In this article I want to set forth as equally scriptural the principle that the church must choose its own elders.

God's decision/the church's choice

And right here we are faced with a paradox. If God in effect says who should and who should not exercise rule over his church, then in what sense are the members of the church permitted to make their own choice? Here is the answer: God qualifies men with spiritual gifts; but the church must learn how to recognize those men so qualified and then must proceed to set them apart to the holy office of elder.

9

It should be clear as day that a very large share of the blame for misrule in our churches must be charged to the failure of congregations to select only God's chosen men. There is so much eagerness on the part of congregations—especially those that are new and expanding—to have what they deem an adequacy of ruling elders; as a result, they frequently fail to study both the Word of God and the men of the church. Consequently, they rush headlong to choose those whom they view as the best available and thrust into office men whom God has not really called.

The problem is aggravated by the fact that so few men will openly seek the office of ruling elder, and thus fail to prepare themselves for this high office. It is quite different in the case of those seeking the pastorate. The latter are often driven by a sense of the divine call; they undergo years of costly training; they are licensed as probationers to make a trial of their gifts to preach the gospel. Then, after the training and the trials, they may be ordained to the office—*but not until the church has given testimony that these men actually possess gifts for the ministry.* Even here mistakes occur, but not with the frequency of those we make in ordaining ruling elders.

The situation in regard to ruling elders is quite different. Here the office tends to seek the man. Even after it has appeared to find him, the man must be persuaded that God wants him in the office. Consequently, the congregation often learns to its sorrow that it has persuaded men to run for the office whom God has not sent. It would have been better that the church consulted less its own eagerness and more the man's own reluctance!

Desiring the office of elder

What is the answer? First, the male members of the church ought more readily to ask themselves whether God might possibly want them to be elders. While I intend to deal with the qualifications for the eldership at a later point, yet we should note here what Paul wrote to Timothy: "It is a true saying, If any man desire the office of a bishop [elder], he desireth a good work" (1 Timothy 3:1). It is *not* wrong to desire the eldership! A man, full of a desire to serve Christ in his church, will then examine himself and study to grow up into that maturity which is in Christ. And so, when there is need for him, he will be ready to serve, and the church's choosing will be far less hazardous.

The other side of the solution of this problem lies in increasing the discernment of the congregation. In Hebrews 5:14, those to whom the epistle is addressed are reproved for a lack of discernment: "When for the time ye ought to be teachers, ye have need that one teach you again which be the first principles of the oracles of God." More positively, John exhorts his readers to "try the spirits" (1 John 4:1-6). That is, they were to learn to test the men who came to them professing to be men of God to see whether they were actuated by the Spirit of Christ or the spirit of Antichrist.

Similarly, John exhorts "the elect lady" to refuse hospitality to those who came not holding the true doctrine of Christ (2 John 10, 11). All that needs to be added here is simply this: Does the Head of the church lay upon the members the requirement that they be discerners of men and of doctrines? Does he require us to discern which men can fulfill the doctrines of God in the use of the means of grace?

More directly, the Scriptures set forth the first prerequisite for the eldership: "A bishop then must be blameless" (1 Timothy 3:2). And who is to judge of his blamelessness if not the congregation in which he belongs and over which he is to rule? "Moreover," Paul says in verse 7, "he must have a good report of them which are without." It is obviously the congregation's prerogative and duty to discover and approve this man's reputation so that he may be a worthy representative of Christ both in the church and toward the world.

Again Paul entreats believers to "know them which labour among you, and are over you in the Lord, and admonish you; and to esteem them" (1 Thessalonians 5:12, 13). It would certainly appear that this knowledge and esteem must be present *before* the man is elevated to office. It would be both impossible and improper to grant esteem where no esteem is warranted.

This is the crux of the whole matter. It is a high privilege to be allowed to choose one's own spiritual rulers, and abuse of that privilege exacts a fearful price. A good com-

11

parison is the privilege a Christian woman has to choose her own husband. She wants to be in submission to him; but there are some men (including some Christian men!) to whom submission is hard to give. It therefore behooves her to take great care what man she would marry. If she chooses hastily and unwisely, she has only herself to blame! So also in the church's choice of her elders.

The church's right to choose

Do congregations really have this power of choice from Scripture? Strange as it may seem, there is very little direct evidence to that effect. We know from Scripture that the whole institution of the eldership was carried over into the New Testament church from Old Testament origins (including the pattern of the synagog as we see it in the Gospels and Acts).

But even here there is no clear guide as to how elders were chosen. Christ himself commissioned the original twelve. But in the first instance of other men being set apart for office we do have a clear scriptural guide.

In Acts 6:1-8 we read about the dissension that arose over inequity in the daily division of food between the Jewish-speaking and the Greek-speaking widows of the Jerusalem church. The apostles declared that their primary duty—the preaching of the Word of God—should not be interrupted by serving tables. "Wherefore, brethren, look ye out among you seven men of honest report, full of the Holy Ghost and wisdom, whom we may appoint over this business" (verse 3).

Notice that the apostles instructed the congregation to find these men. The church was to make the selection. The apostles themselves would ordain ("appoint") the men, and presumably reserved the right to veto an unwise choice. Nevertheless, it is the body of believers who were to take the initiative in choosing their own officers. This principle has been basic to Presbyterian church government ever since.

The congregation must not only choose its spiritual leaders, but it must choose them wisely. And wisdom is available to those believers who seek it from the Word and in prayer to him who "giveth to all men liberally, and upbraideth not." It follows that, to avoid laying hands on

12

any man "suddenly" (1 Timothy 5:22), the church must have true knowledge of the character and gifts of every man she would put in the place of rule.

That the church has not always done this is painfully evident to all who observe the life of the church today. It would seem that at least a year of observing would be a reasonable minimum before a church elevates a man to the office of elder. This is true even in the case of those who have ruled in other congregations. Paul did not immediately ordain elders in the newly established churches of his first missionary journey—not even those who were synagog elders already. Only after they had all been established did he return to these congregations to ordain elders in each one. For some of these the waiting period may well have been as much as a year. Not only that, these men were chosen and ordained with prayer and fasting (Acts 14:21-23; cf. 13:3).

Our ascended Lord has been providing gifted men for his church since Pentecost. He can be depended on to continue the supply till he comes again. These gifts should be prayed for, developed, and encouraged on the part of men in the church. This is God's way.

Recently I heard a sermon in which the preacher spoke of ministers and others who were over-zealous that their particular gifts be recognized and given a place in the church. The preacher said that there was no need to worry about that; if anyone has gifts, and uses his opportunities to exercise these gifts, in due time the church will recognize them. The man need not make a place for his gifts to be employed; rather, the gifts themselves will make a place for him!

How true this is! A correct attitude for all who serve our sovereign Lord is just this: What I am is really not very important. What is important is that whatever Christ has given me I will make available to him to use where and when and how he chooses. Then I will have all the satisfaction I need, and more honor than I can safely cope with. This is especially true for those whom Christ has gifted and given "for the perfecting of the saints, unto the work of the ministry, unto the edifying of the body of Christ."

3

LABORING IN THEIR CALLING

I like the word "session" (which means "a sitting together"). In Presbyterian churches this is the common name for the body of elders of a local congregation. Among their duties the highest is that of sitting together as a court of the Lord Jesus Christ, ruling for him over the affairs of his flock.

The work of the undershepherds

The trouble is that many men who sit on sessions seem to think that sitting is all that elders have to do. They forget that elders, as Christ's undershepherds, must also *stand* to minister to the saints; they must *walk* (and sometimes *run*) to seek Christ's wandering sheep; they must *kneel* daily to lift up the flock before the throne of grace in prayer!

In this article I want to sketch something of the breadth of this holy office. The qualifications for eldership (to be discussed in detail in a later article) can be summed up as basically three: (1) An elder must be a stable, mature Christian; (2) he must possess special gifts for ruling; and (3) he must be "apt to teach" (1 Timothy 3:1-7).

While I shall use for convenience the terminology of "ruling and teaching elder," I believe this distinction is unfortunate. It is readily admitted that "all elders rule"; but the second part of that old saying — "and some elders teach" — is not accurate. Paul tells Timothy that a bishop (elder) must be "apt to teach."* And this applies to all elders without distinction.

---

* Several scholars have argued that "apt to teach" may be a misleading translation of the Greek term *(didaktikos)*. It

14

That some elders today cannot teach is evidence that these men hold an office for which they are not fully qualified. The real distinction within the office of elder would be stated this way: All elders should "rule well"; but some of these are called to "labor in the word and doctrine." Some, in other words, give themselves wholly to laboring in the ministry of the Word of God. (See 1 Timothy 5:17, 18.)

The scope of eldership

The elders as a body (or session) are responsible for guarding the gates of the visible church. They exercise the keys of the kingdom of heaven for binding and loosing (Matthew 16:19; 18:18). It is their duty, ministering in Jesus' name, to pronounce as repentant and justified sinners all who come before them giving credible evidence of being born again to faith in Christ. And to these the elders of the church must minister the sacrament of the Lord's Supper and the sacrament of baptism to them and their children.

In other words, the session is to receive repentant and believing sinners into Christ's church and is to feed them there. But since these believers may stumble and fall into sin, the session must also stand ready to deal with this situation. They may even be forced to acknowledge that their first judgment was in error and finally to put the disobedient and obdurate outside the fold of the Good Shepherd.

It is here that many elders fail. Though they may be men of integrity, yet many times they are either unable or unwilling to render such judgment *for Christ*. Too often, in admitting and disciplining members under their care, they are moved to judge according to their feelings of like or dislike toward the individuals concerned, and thus become judges of evil thoughts (James 2:4).

This failure is in two areas: (1) These elders fail to realize that their decisions are *in Christ's name and in his*

---

may mean "able to be taught" rather than "able to teach." But the need for the ruling elder to be able to teach does not depend on this phrase. Since all rule in the church is "ministerial and declarative," and not despotic and co-ercive, every church ruler must be ready to minister the truth, to declare it — to *teach* it to the flock.

15

stead. It is his church, not theirs. It is to him they must answer for their use of the keys. True, they constitute a court; but they must always realize that there is a higher Court to which all cases will be appealed in the end! What then will be their reward when called to give an account of their stewardship to the Head of the church?

(2) These elders may also fail to rule well due to incompetence in the knowledge, use and application of Holy Scripture to the persons and cases under consideration. A good test of whether or not a particular session rules well can be found in whether or not their actions in this area are done with a near unanimity. Surely there is room for divergence of opinion among brethren in such decisions. But when basic questions of doctrine or life are before a session, these elders ought to be able to speak with one voice simply because the Word of God speaks with one voice on the great matters of faith and life!

Elders as individual rulers

The exercise of rule by the session rests upon and grows out of the activity of each individual elder as he goes in and out among the people. The activity of a session as it sits to rule is a high and holy calling. But that activity should never be an "ivory tower" sort of thing.

When the elders are "up there" in session, their minds and hearts must be fully aware of all that goes on "down there" where the church lives in the world. These men must have the pulse of the people if they are to rule well in session. But how do elders get that way? Through the labors of teaching, of teaching the Word, exhorting the people, admonishing *"publicly and from house to house"* (Acts 20:20).

Yes, *all* elders have a public ministry of the Word. This is not to suppose that they have equal shares in that ministry. Some are not as gifted as others in public exhortation, be it Sunday school teaching, conducting Bible classes or prayer meetings, or "lay" preaching. But every elder ought to have some ability to communicate the Word of God on a one-to-one basis at the very least.

The man who is totally lacking in this ability ought not to be an elder (Titus 1:9). In fact, I would stress that every session of any size ought to have at least one ruling elder with talents for preaching so that he can fill the pulpit from time to time. Certainly those with evident gifts in this area should be encouraged to develop those gifts fully.

The elders and the pastor

We still haven't exhausted the duties of the ruling elders in this area of the public ministry of the Word. For the elders of the church "should have particular regard to the doctrine and conduct of the minister of the Word, in order that the church may be edified, and may manifest itself as the pillar and ground of the truth" (as stated in the warrant for the office of elder in the *Directory for Worship* of the Orthodox Presbyterian Church, Ch. VI, B, 2).

In other words, the ruling elders should encourage, advise, and give constructive criticism to the pastor in his role as chief teaching elder for the congregation. The pulpit can be a lonely place. The pastor who stands there from week to week without such support from his fellow elders is called to bear a burden too heavy for one pair of shoulders!

There is need at this point to sound a serious warning. It sometimes happens that members of the congregation will come to one or more of the elders, expressing feelings of resentment or disapproval of the pastor's preaching or of his ministry in general. This is not wrong in itself. Some pastors appear rather unapproachable to those who sit in the pews. Still, everything depends on how the elders handle such expressions of concern.

If an elder readily agrees with the complaints, the word will get around and he will soon become the rally-point for dissension and division. He must shun this role! If the criticisms are trivial, he should deal with them from the position of solidarity with the pastor. If he cannot resolve the problems, it becomes his duty to bring the dissidents and the pastor together in a prayerful effort to heal what would otherwise become a breach in the peace of the church. In fact, procedures to deal with such possibilities ought to be worked out in the session and agreed upon *before* troubles of this sort surface! In short, elders are to be healers, not inflicters, of wounds in the body of Christ.

17

The elders and the people

To put the matter differently, the ruling elders need to be alert for seeds of dissension within the church family as a whole, that they might be healers of incipient discord at all times. When any elder is unable to heal a developing problem singly, he must immediately bring the problem to the attention of the session before the whole church is hopelessly torn asunder.

We might visualize this matter by picturing two concentric circles, a small one within a larger. The smaller circle is the session, existing within the larger circumference of the whole congregation. Within the smaller circle there should be no division or dissension, if the elders are truly and preeminently men of God and able to apply the Scripture to every area of life. But within the larger circle there are bound to be problems from time to time.

Elders who have their eyes and ears open (and at the same time are walking with God) can deal personally with most of these, always attempting to guide the brethren into a scriptural resolution of the problems. But when personal efforts fail, the problem must come before the whole session, into the smaller circle, where it can receive the attention of the whole body of rulers. If dealt with here promptly and scripturally, there is no problem in any church that cannot be resolved to the glory of God and the edifying of God's people, even in those cases where excision of an obdurate member becomes necessary.

Ruling is teaching

It is quite unrealistic to separate the teaching from the ruling function in the work of the elder. All elders rule by teaching — and teach by ruling — even though at times they may be concentrating chiefly on one aspect. Even in the extreme of judicial discipline there is a teaching ministry, since nothing should be done except as the need for it arises out of the Word of God.

For this reason elders must stay close to those over whom they rule, even as they must stay close to the Word of him for whom they do rule. The elders need to be personally and intimately acquainted with the lives of the members

18

of the flock. The teaching elder should remind the congregation that elders are representatives of the Lord and are to be heard, submitted to, and obeyed in the Lord (cf. Hebrews 13:17, 17).

An excellent system for this purpose (and one with a long history among Presbyterians) is to assign a proportionate share of the church's families to each ruling elder, to whom and for whom he is responsible to minister. It will be his duty to visit in their homes, to exhort them personally on all sorts of questions when he discerns their need for it. They in turn will be taught to expect this sort of ministry, even to seek it out when they feel a need for it.

A family's special overseer must be often in that home to rejoice with members of the family in times of joy, to weep with them in times of sorrow. It will soon be obvious to every member of the church that his elder-overseer has him personally on his heart, bearing him up before the throne of grace day in and day out. If every ruling elder were to become effective in such a ministry it could never be said of any — as I have heard it said of some — "I could never feel free to bring my problems to him!"

Let the life of every man of God be transparently the life of one who cares! And caring costs. But when the Chief Shepherd calls on his undershepherds to give an account of their ministry, every man worthy of his calling to rule will reply, "I cared for thy flock, for some with joy and for others with grief." Let us all, elders and people, take stock of this fact and learn how we all ought to behave ourselves in the house of God.

"If a man desire the office of a bishop," said Paul to Timothy, "he desireth a good work." Good work, in any field, is seldom easy. Good work will often call for weary hours of plodding, for long night vigils, for heartaches and tears. God give us men who will work and strive and pray and weep for the flock of God that he purchased with the blood of his Son!

4

THE SUBMISSION DUE TO THEM

In any society of free men, the rule of law is only possible as long as the vast majority of its members are habitually law-abiding. When respect for authority breaks down to the extent that larger and larger numbers defy existing rule, the only remaining alternative to anarchy is a police state. And when this state of affairs prevails, men are no longer free.

The same is true of the church. All those received as communicant members of a Presbyterian church must take this or a similar vow: "Do you agree to submit in the Lord to the government of this church and, in case you should be found delinquent in doctrine or life, to heed its discipline?" (*Directory for Worship* of the Orthodox Presbyterian Church, V, 5). A close look at this question reveals two things that everyone taking this vow has bound himself to do:

1. The newly received member has said that he accepts the form of Presbyterian church government, at least at the local level, as agreeable to the government of Christ as Head of his church because he agrees to submit to the government of "this church" *in the Lord*.

2. Even more significant is his agreement to submit "to the *government* of this church." The government has a particular form to which the communicant assents; but government is more than a form. The government of any church *is* the men who rule over it in the name of Christ.

In Part 3 of this series, I attempted to show that, while only God *makes* elders, yet he has not withheld from his people the gift of discerning what men are so gifted and spiritually equipped to rule over them. I also pointed out that the obvious reason why this choice must remain with the members of the congregation is that it is they who must yield them that scriptural submission. Therefore the members of the local congregation, above all others, have a personal interest in choosing those to whom they must submit!

The yoke of Christ

When one joins a truly scriptural church he takes upon himself the yoke of Christ. Jesus said, "Take my yoke upon you and learn of me; for I am meek and lowly in heart" (Matthew 11:29). In this our Lord said two things pertinent to our discussion:

1. In plain language he said that he himself wore a yoke in lowliness and meekness. What was that yoke? It was doing his Father's will in that great ministry in which he "humbled himself, and became obedient unto . . . the death of the cross" (Philippians 2:8). Included in this yoke was his submission to Joseph and Mary in his boyhood home at Nazareth—most humbling for the Son of God! (See Luke 2:49, 51.) He even paid his temple tax and yielded meekly to the judging of Caiaphas the high priest during his trial before the Sanhedrin (Matthew 26:63). In all of this our Lord showed an amazing example of meekness under his Father's yoke, even to the God-given authority of sinful men who were over him as a human being and a son of Israel!

2. But it is his yoke that Jesus invites us to take and wear as our own with the same lowly submission that he demonstrated. That is the meaning of the words, "Take my yoke upon you and learn of me." And what is that yoke? Surely it includes conscientious and glad submission to those gifted men that—along with the giving of the Spirit himself— our Lord poured out upon the church from his exalted place at the Father's right hand (cf. Ephesians 4:8, 12). Make no mistake about it: those pastor-teachers are empowered to rule us! (See 1 Timothy 3:5; Hebrews 13:17; 1 Peter 5:1-4.)

Here is where we can see a crying need for reform in our Reformed churches. There is too often a gross failure to take the rule of elders seriously. While we are aware that it is the duty of elders to rule and to teach, we seem to be reluctant to agree that it is our duty to obey and to learn. This deficiency of serious regard for the prerogatives of the elders arises from two things: a failure in the exercise of *personal* oversight of the flock by the elders, and a failure of consistent submission to the official preaching of the Word from the pulpit. Let's take a look at these in order

Personal oversight by the elders

I have already dealt with the subject of the ruling elder's responsibility to exercise ongoing and personal oversight of the individual members and families of the church. But this is not being regularly done in a great many of our churches. And the failure has contributed to an attitude on the part of church members that personal oversight is only given in unusual cases. Consequently, when one elder (or perhaps two together) calls on a family for a formal visit there is a tensing up that greatly inhibits the elder's ministry to that family. If succeeding calls are infrequent, this tenseness and foreboding never leave the situation.

What is needed is a great deal of loving and patient instruction. The elders first need to be instructed as to how they may bring their visitation ministry faithfully and disarmingly. The whole church needs periodic pulpit exhortation so that the visitation of elders will come to be accepted and then welcomed as an extension of Christ's own loving care for his people. It seems to me that presbyteries and other agencies of Reformed denominations might well sponsor conferences and workshops dealing with this.

Let me say again that the first reason that congregations tend to hold a light attitude toward the rule of elders over them is due to the lack of persistent, prayerful, and loving exercise of personal oversight by the elders themselves. I long for the day that members of our churches will come to welcome, and expect as their due, regular and frequent visits from their ruling elders that are truly spiritual, catechetical, and pastoral in the finest sense of that word.

Submission to official preaching

The other area crying for reform in our Reformed churches is the lack of conscious and consistent submission by confessing members to the official preaching of the Word from the pulpits. In New Testament times believers had no option as to which congregation of worshipping Christians they were privileged to attend. There was only one church within walking distance. Failure to sit under the ministry of the Word in that particular assembly meant exclusion from the public worship of God.

Today we have hundreds of churches to choose from. And not all of these are apostate. There is even a wide choice in some areas of churches within the same denomination. Now it has often been said that Americans are "joiners." This is also true of American Christians. We need but little encouragement to join some church. But it is not uncommon, in our best churches, to find someone missing in his own church only to discover that he is now going to the church down the street that recently called a new pastor. It never seems to have crossed this church member's mind that he has any obligation to give notice of his intention to go elsewhere to his own spiritual rulers, much less to give honest reasons for so doing!

I need to be clear on one thing right here. Our duty to the government of our particular church does not forbid the visiting of other churches. There are joint services and special programs where this sort of thing is healthy and helpful to our need for Christian fellowship. Furthermore, there are times when a Christian needs to rethink his relationship to his own church. There are circumstances where one *ought* to change churches. And it is not always necessary to sever one's existing connections before considering another one. But in such cases, the right thing to do is to give notice, with honest reasons, for the contemplated change.

But unadorned "church hopping," pure and simple, is another thing altogether. Here there is evident a lack of submission to the rulers of the church to which one is bound by solemn vows. And this equals a lack of submission to Christ, the Lord of the church. To "agree to submit in the Lord to the government of *this* church" means to accept the total ministry of that particular congregation and the rule of those men raised up by the Lord of the church to teach and rule in that church. To leave the ministry of the Word in that particular congregation, without due cause or notice, is to forsake the ordinance of Christ.

It is Christ who has ordained rule in his church and ordained particular rulers in particular churches. Do you think he will smile upon anyone who takes his ordinances so lightly? Could this not lead to the terrible sin of hardness to the gospel? And should that be the result, is it not a judgment from God?

For any believer who has chosen to worship God as a member of a particular church, all other things being as they should, the official preaching of the pastor of that church is the word of Jesus Christ to that believer. The church member, according to the ordinance of God, owes submission of ears, of mind, and of heart to the content of his pastor's teaching.

Submission to the whole ministry

One other aspect of this same question needs brief mention. There is no alternative "Plan A" or "Plan B" offered to confessing members of Christ's church. It's not as though upon joining the church an option is given of being a "oncer" (Sunday morning only) or a "twicer" (morning *and* evening). Obedient submission is due to the total public ministry of the church within the limits of one's ability to be there.

If the Lord's Day is a whole day, and if two worship services on the Lord's Day are not only according to the need of the people but also an honest approach toward keeping the day holy, then one who is truly submissive to the rule of Christ in his church will want to be present unless prevented by providential circumstances.

Christ does not exercise his rule over the church *im*mediately, but *mediately*. Therefore, he rules his church through those men he has gifted and given to the church for that purpose. Every confessing Christian ought to be under the rule of Christ by placing himself under the rule of the elders of a particular church. To take that rule with lack of seriousness and solemnity is to do despite to the rule of Christ himself! And remember: the fact that these men of God are themselves sinners—which they are—no more relieves us from submission to them than the boy Jesus was relieved from submitting to Joseph and Mary while living in their home at Nazareth.

5

THEIR SCRIPTURAL QUALIFICATIONS

I have purposely refrained until now from discussing at length the qualifications for the eldership. Of course, passing reference to these has been made, but no more than the context demanded. This was done so that we might get a balanced view of the whole forest before examining the greatest tree in it. Elder qualifications represent that great tree amidst the forest of related matters that make up the total complex of government in Christ's church.

An elder must be a *man*

Happily, we have the scriptural qualifications listed in an orderly way in 1 Timothy 3:2-7, with some further enlargement in Titus 1:7-9. But before attempting to expound these passages, some matters of a preliminary and essential nature must be discussed.

The first of these is that elders must be men, and only men. This fact needs to be reaffirmed in these days when many Reformed and Presbyterian churches (not all of which are apostate) are buckling under pressure to admit women to the ordained teacher-ruler office.

Scripture is unequivocal on this point. Even if we were to allow that I Corinthians 14:34 ("Let your women keep silence in the churches . . .") is speaking to a peculiar local problem, yet Paul supports this strict prohibition on more general principles of Scripture (". . . as also saith the law" —meaning the Old Testament).

To understand Paul's appeal to the Old Testament law, look at 1 Corinthians 11:3-9. Here Paul grounds his asser-

25

tion that man is to rule the woman (not to be ruled by her) in the very order of their creation. "The head of (i.e., ruler over) every man is Christ, and the head of the woman is the man." Man's positional (*not* essential) superiority over the woman rests on the fact that God made the woman of man's own substance, and made her *for* the man.

Paul leaves the question beyond quibble in 1 Timothy 2:9-15. (And this is the first of the pastoral epistles, which lay down permanent rules for the government and conduct of the church.) Why does Paul say, ". . . if a *man* desire the office of a bishop, he desireth a good work" (3:2)? Because he had just written, *"I suffer not a woman to teach, or to usurp authority over the man."* And to make doubly sure he is stating an ageless principle rather than a temporary expedient, Paul refers again to the creation order.

The apostle gives as ground for this principle the priority of the man over the woman in creation, *and* the priority of the woman over the man in sin. The latter fact enforces the former, just because it is a reversal of the order of the created nature of the man and the woman; this only accentuates the rightness of the creation order contrasted with man's tendency to rebel against the will of God as revealed in what he made them.

It ill behooves the church of Jesus Christ in this still-sinful world to fly in the teeth of the will of God revealed in his creation ordinance, especially in the choice of those who are exalted to the position of Christ's assistant restorers of what sin has destroyed. After all, is it not absurd to hold that *God* makes men bishops, and then to elevate to that high position those to whom God has forbidden the exercise of those ruling functions in his inspired Word?

An elder *must* be ———

Another preliminary general consideration has to do with one word with which Paul begins his list of qualifications in 1 Timothy 3:2-7: "A bishop (or elder) *must* be blameless . . ." Both in the English and the Greek, this little word *must* has the same force that it has in John 3:7, when Jesus said to Nicodemus, "Ye *must* be born again."

In other words, the Scripture is speaking (in both cases) of an *essential qualification.* New birth is mandatory for those who would enter the kingdom of God; blamelessness is absolutely required for those who would assume the office of the elder. There is no option; the candidate must be blameless.

Now the *must* belongs to more than just being blameless. Paul did not mean to say that "a bishop must be blameless, and it's a good idea — though not absolutely essential — that he also be such-and-such else also." This strong little word *must* applies equally to all the fourteen qualifications that follow. And again, we must remember that it is God who makes men bishops; neither Paul, nor Timothy, nor today's church has the least power or right to change the qualifications God has set forth. Our business is to observe the workings of grace in the lives of twice-born men, and to judge of their fitness for the office on the basis of *all* the qualifications given in Scripture.

These qualities will never be found in any but sinners. Not even elders are fully sanctified. Hence we should not expect that all elders will have all these qualifications in full development or perfect balance. One man may excel in one or more, whereas another's excellence appears where the first man's gifts (though present) do not especially excel.

This underscores the wisdom of Scripture's requirement that the church be ruled by a plurality of elders. "In the multitude of counselors there is safety" (Proverbs 24:6). I have observed, both on the sessional and presbyterial level, that small bodies tend to make erratic decisions. The very variety of gifts possessed among a session of elders is a matter for praise to God who stoops to take sinners into partnership with him in the work of his kingdom on earth!

QUALIFICATIONS REQUIRED FOR RULE

Can we discern a pattern in the list of qualifications for the office of elder as laid down by Paul in his letters to Timothy and Titus? I believe we can. There are fourteen of them in 1 Timothy 3:2-7; numbers one through seven, twelve and fourteen are positive in form, while numbers eight through eleven and thirteen are negative.

Two of these positive qualifications stand out from all the rest. We speak of *ruling* and *teaching* elders. Accordingly, gifts for rule and teaching stand out above the others, reflecting the very nature of the work that elders must do. The other qualifications reflect the character of the men who perform these functions. So, gifts for teaching and rule are in a sense special, whereas the others are general.

These more general qualifications make clear that those who teach and rule must be mellowed, mature Christians. In fact, the very term *elder* says as much of itself. Nevertheless, Paul does not leave us to deduce these things from the terms *elder* or *bishop;* he spells them out for all to see.

The elder must first be blameless. This cannot mean sinless. Rather, we are looking for a man who, though indeed a sinner, habitually strives to walk by the rule of God's Word. A blameless man will not be found doing what he knows is plainly wrong. If, through ignorance or a moment when his guard is down, he does sin, he will repent instantly upon his awareness of having sinned against God. Should he give place to sinful anger (and who has never done so?), he will not let the sun go down on his wrath (Ephesians 4:26). If he wrongs another in any way, he will not need to be prodded to make right the wrong he has done. In a word, he will always walk as one who is aware that men will judge Jesus Christ by him. And it will be his prayer that men will *see* Jesus through him.

The elder must be the husband of one wife. Many have differed as to the precise meaning of these words. Must an elder be a married man? I do not think so. Paul, in virtue of his being an apostle, was also an elder (1 Peter 5:1). Yet Paul was not married, and pleaded good cause for his living in the single state. No church ought to refuse to ordain a man to the eldership simply because he is unmarried. I hasten to add, however, that I would not want to preside over a session made up entirely of bachelors!

The real force of the words is that elders must be chosen from among men who have only one wife at a time. If this statement sounds strange in our ears, we need to be reminded that in times ancient and modern the gospel has been preached to and received by those who do not live in strict monogamy. Whatever else may be said of such a situation, we are forbidden to look for rulers for the church from among those having more than one wife.

A man who has married for the second time (his first wife having died) may surely be an elder. The Bible knows nothing of man-contrived super-sainthood. Elders must be saints, and relatively mature ones at that; but super-saints, never! "It is not good that the man should be alone," the Lord God said at the beginning (Genesis 2:18). And Scripture fully expects that most elders will be married to one wife and thankful to God for having made it so.

But what of the divorced man, whether remarried or not? Can he be an elder? The answer depends on many factors beyond the scope of this study. Satisfactory answers must be found to questions such as these: Was the divorce and (possible) remarriage accomplished before the man was converted? Were there biblical grounds for the divorce? Even if there were, did he contribute secondarily to the breakup of the original marriage? The least that can be said here is that all the more pains ought to be taken in discerning the tokens of a divine call to this man before he is admitted to the sacred office. And it is always wise, for prospective elders and for others also, to secure from the church itself a decree of divorce if that is justifiable, so that the good name of Christ may not be needlessly sullied before the world.

The elder must be vigilant, sober, and of good behavior. Due to the overlap of meaning in these three adjectives, they are better taken together. *Vigilant* may be understood as meaning "sober with respect to the use of wine." But since Paul also speaks of this matter later, it is better taken to mean "serious-minded" or "pertaining to one who is a down-to-earth realist, one not given to flights of fancy or living in a dream world."

The word translated *sober* definitely refers to soundness of mind, prudence, self-control. In Mark 5:15, the demoniac from whom our Lord cast out the legion of demons was afterwards found "sitting, and clothed, and *in his right mind*," this last phrase being closely related to the word in our text.

Of good behavior means one who exercises that sort of self-control that enables him to manage all the outward affairs of life. All three terms taken together mean that every elder ought to be one who has a good mind, able to look at things objectively and fairly. He must be able to rise above his own feelings about anyone, above his own prejudices. In a word, he must be a man of good mental discipline, able to control his own emotions. He must be one who, under modern pressures, does not easily panic or go to pieces. He must be able so to handle his personal affairs as to find time for everything that has a legitimate claim upon his time and attention. He must order his business, social, family, and kingdom affairs on the principle of first things first, last things last, and frivolous and useless things never. He must become skillful in "redeeming the time" the Lord gives him.

Let us consider one more positive qualification for the eldership in this installment. **The elder must be given to hospitality.** We can hardy overemphasize this. Mere hospitality had a most useful and necessary place in Bible times. The times have indeed changed so that mere hospitality may not be as needful as it once was, with motels and restaurants available to all. Nevertheless, our modern culture is giving way to the extent that mere hospitality is coming more and more to be a useful means of evangelism and nurture in Christian fellowship.

But hospitality does not mean just an open door to one's home. The hospitable man is one whose heart is first open to the lonely, the rejected, the alien among men of all kinds and in all conditions. Even if a man has a home and the means to extend outward hospitality, or even if he goes so far as to provide hotel accommodations at his own expense, and yet the man lacks a loving heart in all of this, he fails the test of biblical hospitality (1 Corinthians 13:2).

Hospitality is really a matter of faith, the faith without which no man can please God. It is a faith shown by its works, the faith of the "good Samaritan" in our Lord's parable. This man was truly given to hospitality, to willingness to offer help because of his concern for the one in need. Elders of the church, and all who aspire to that "good work," "Go, and do thou likewise!"

6

THEIR SCRIPTURAL QUALIFICATIONS (2)

Timothy, an elder, was called by Paul a man of God. That is, having first been created a man in the natural sense, he was recreated and equipped spiritually to be God's man in a special sense (1 Timothy 6:11; 2 Timothy 3:17). Elders are made by God, not men. It is God who gives the gifts and works the grace in their lives so that, as gifted men, they are fitted for the teaching–ruling office in his church. But this is not automatic. The church must be taught to recognize these gifts in God's men. Failure to learn and recognize these qualifications leads to costly mistakes.

In the previous article I wrote about certain *general positive* qualifications as listed in 1 Timothy 3:2. I pointed out that all qualifications except two (those having to do with teaching and rule) are really what we ought to find in every mature Christian. These are the marks of the developed Christian. The remaining qualifications may be grouped as: (1) *general negative;* (2) *special,* and (3) *remaining general* qualifications.

GENERAL NEGATIVE QUALIFICATIONS

The negative qualifications for an elder are listed in 1 Timothy 3:3 and Titus 1:7. Paul tells Timothy that a bishop (elder) must *not be given to wine.* This is not to forbid the use of wine, but says the elder must not be addicted to it. In other words, God's men must have full control over their appetites, especially the appetite for strong drink.

In our present culture an elder might well fulfill this

requirement by abstaining totally from alcoholic beverages. True, total abstinence must not be made a test of either fellowship or office. But the office bearer at least must so conduct himself as to be above reproach in what is one of the most serious problems of the day. All his bodily appetites must be under the control of a mind and will that is itself fully under the control of the Christian's Lord. For myself, I have no idea how well I might control the use of alcohol; I have therefore chosen to remove it from me as a potential problem.

Furthermore, we do no violence to this Scripture teaching if we draw the inference that habitual use of drugs is also forbidden for elders. Whatever use of whatever drug we elect to take *must* be under full and vigilant control. Our bodies are the temples of the Holy Spirit. Paul himself testifies to the subduing of his own body lest, having preached to others, he might become a castaway (cf. 1 Corinthians 3:16, 17 and 9:27).

Not a stubborn arrogant man

Paul goes on to say that an elder must be *no striker.* To Titus he says that the elder must be *not self-willed.* And he adds (in 1 Timothy) that the elder must be *patient* (according to the order of the more authentic Greek text).

Now it would seem that Paul has most in mind the tendency to mental rather than physical violence. It adds up, then, to this: An elder must not be self-willed, stubborn, arrogant, or overbearing. And sadly, many such men have occupied the office—though they often describe themselves as "firm and uncompromising."

How do we spot this type of person? Look for the man who, when his mind is made up on some difficult and complex subject, takes the attitude that anyone who questions his conclusions is questioning God himself! Somehow people of this stripe seem to have a pipeline to heaven that the rest of us have missed. What is more, when their minds are made up they are not only adamant but positively overweening. To reason with them, or even work with them, is a hopeless task. They manifest the spirit of "Diotrephes, who loveth to have the preeminence" (3 John 9).

Paul's alternative is the gentle, patient man, the one who

is fairminded, fully willing and able to understand a different point of view—even when he disagrees with it. He is firm when he knows he stands squarely on the Word. But he is always open to being convinced from the same Word that his opinion is wrong, and when convinced he does not find it hard to say he was wrong.

Not lusting after wealth

The last negative qualification is that the elder must not be *greedy of filthy lucre* (1 Timothy 3:3), or *given to filthy lucre* (Titus 1:7). Money, with other earthly possessions, may not be so highly prized as to hinder in any way the calling to follow Christ.

An elder may be a successful businessman, even a man of wealth. But he must not be a lover of money or a slave to wealth. He may not serve mammon ever so slightly (Matthew 6:24). The consuming desire for wealth must be far from him. And if he is wealthy, he must not "trust in uncertain riches" (1 Timothy 6:9, 17). It is highly inconceivable that any man today would seek the office of elder as a means to acquire wealth. Rather, every candidate for this high office ought to be ready to be made poorer for his pains!

The King James Version includes two additional qualifications (in 1 Timothy 3:3): "not a brawler, not covetous." The latter is really covered under the previous stipulation, and the former is stated as *not soon angry* in Titus 1:7. An elder needs not only to be in full control of his bodily appetites but also of his emotions. Some men express anger with wild tongues, others with wild fists. The former are the greater menace, but neither has a place of rule or teaching in the house of God.

We are not looking for supine milquetoasts. We need strong men to whom to commit the rule of Christ's church. But they must be men whom the Holy Spirit has tamed and brought under the yoke of Christ. God has no work in his church for emotional outlaws.

SPECIAL QUALIFICATIONS

All the qualifications discussed so far have been general ones. The elder, by his very title, must be a mature Christian. And this is the sum of all we have said. But there are two special qualifications that stand out above the rest. Without these two special gifts, an elder would be in the same category with a blind artist or a vocalist who can't carry a tune. And these gifts must not only be possessed by an elder, but he must possess them to an advanced degree.

These special gifts are those of teaching and ruling. Let me say again that these gifts cannot in practice be divided in a man of God. He rules by his teaching, and he teaches in his ruling. They are in him Siamese-twin virtues; severed, they both die. They are like brain and brawn; a brain without some muscle power is useless, but mere brawn with no brain is dangerous. Nevertheless, it is helpful and feasible to consider each separately and we need also to keep in mind that the two are never found in perfect balance except in the perfect Man, Christ Jesus.

The man apt to teach

An elder, Paul says, must be *apt to teach* (1 Timothy 3:2). This phrase in Greek might be translated "teachable." Yet the active sense seems more in line with Paul's similar instruction to Titus (1:9). The elder must be adept at "holding fast the faithful word as he hath been taught, that he may be able by sound doctrine [teaching] to exhort and convince the gainsayers."

Now this sentence includes the idea that the elder must be a good learner—"teachable"—since he can't teach others what he hasn't learned for himself. Yet the thrust of the words is on the elder's ability to set forth sound doctrine.

This teaching function must be done with a view to its *application to the needs of men.* Nor do I think we are to understand Paul's words narrowly here as though he only had gainsayers in mind. Rather, we do no violence to Scripture if we paraphrase the thought to mean, "that he may be able to exhort and convince *even* the gainsayers." If he can convince the all but unteachable, he should be capable of teaching anyone else.

I hasten to add that an elder need not be a gifted public speaker, or an able teacher of the Bible to large groups, though both these gifts are highly desirable. But at the very least, *an elder must be able to deal with people on a one-to-one basis, applying the Word to the needs of the individual.*

34

The man able to rule

Again, an elder must be gifted in the art of ruling. This is related to the requirement that he be "the husband of one wife." Ordinarily we are to look for a man who "ruleth well his own house, having his children in subjection with all gravity" (1 Timothy 3:4). We've already said that this is not to be understood as barring all bachelors from the office of elder. Their ability to rule may be judged by their business activities, or their leadership qualities, or their ability in teaching both in day schools or Sunday school.

But the most natural way to prove a man's gifts for ruling is to observe how he handles himself in his own home and among his own family members. Paul had this in mind when he wrote to Titus about elders "having faithful children not accused of riot or unruly." How do a man's children behave toward him in the home? Is there a proper balance of fairness and firmness and affection evident there? Do the children show a good attitude elsewhere toward authority? Are they always made aware that they, as a family, are all under the lordship of Christ and his Word?

And what about the man's wife? Is she also subject to her own husband in the Lord? Does he have the mind of Christ toward her (Ephesians 5:21–28)? Or is her tongue so far from the "law of kindness" (Proverbs 31:26) that it "setteth on fire the course of nature, and is set on fire of hell" (James 3:6)? God's men are called upon to pass most rigorous tests!

Nevertheless, we must guard against adding to God's requirements as much as taking away from them. It is sadly true that the children of some very godly men grow to an adulthood of unbelief and rebellion against God. Is a man to be disqualified because his children have not been born again? I think not. God, not man, holds the key to the hearts of all who were born in sin. It is not always in us to say *why* one and not another person is saved. It may be the fault of the pastor, or the church as a whole, and not solely a parental failure that results in a child's not turning to Christ.

All that Paul requires is that these children, while in the home, are to be in submission to their father, and that they do not behave in the community so as to be a scandal against the name of Christ.

And what if it is the wife who fails to be a follower of Christ? The husband is not necessarily to be faulted for this. To what degree does his unbelieving wife undermine the father's role as Christ's viceregent to his children? And to what degree does her unbelief negate his influence in the community and among God's people? These are the questions to be asked and weighed carefully.

As complex as the application of such rules may seem under certain life situations, there is no excuse for our setting them aside or taking them with anything less than the utmost seriousness. The flock of Christ is too dearly bought for us to afflict it with the rule of men less gifted and diligent than the Word of God specifies!

It ought to be the constant prayer of the church that her Lord and Head will raise up such men to teach and rule his people. And let those who aspire to this office set foot upon that narrow path with fear and trembling. They are not, in themselves, sufficient for these things; their sufficiency can only be from the Lord, who dearly loves his bride the church.

7

THEIR SCRIPTURAL QUALIFICATIONS (3)

The Holy Spirit hath made you bishops [elders], *to feed the church of the Lord which he purchased with his own blood* (Acts 20:28, *ASV*).

The Holy Spirit makes men elders. The inward call of the Spirit must be verified by the outward call of the church. Therefore, elders ought to be chosen by those over whom they are to bear rule (Acts 6.:3). Nevertheless, they may not be put in possession of the office except by the laying on of hands by those already in office (Acts 6:3; 13:23; 1 Timothy 5:22; 2 Timothy 2:2).

Nor has the Spirit left us in the dark as to what are the marks of the Spirit-made man. The qualifications are carefully listed in 1 Timothy 3:2-7 and Titus 1:6-9. It is noteworthy that, "A bishop *must* be blameless . . . . etc." *All* the qualifications must be met, though not in the fullest possible degree of development. All these gifts must be fully discernible in every man upon whom the hands of ordination are to be laid. This is especially important in the two primary areas that mark out the scope of the elders' labors—that of teaching and of ruling.

Two qualifications still remain to be considered (1 Timothy 3:6, 7). They differ in form, but they belong together, being more than an afterthought since these alone are hedged by serious warning and are related to the workings of the devil. Let us look at these requirements as they stand, and then at the dire consequence of their neglect.

A bishop must not be a novice

"A bishop then must be . . . *not a novice.*" The meaning is clear. An elder must not be a new Christian, a babe in the faith. Isn't that the reason for calling him an *elder?* He must be mature in faith and of approved behavior before the church. That is why Paul cautioned Timothy to "lay hands suddenly on no man" (1 Timothy 5:22). In other words, the Spirit-made men whom the ascended Lord gives to his church "for the perfecting of the saints" must not be set apart for that office until the Spirit has prepared them for it.

It is not that there will be no more growing in grace for an elder, but the Spirit's work in him must be complete to the point that he is "no more a child, tossed to and fro with every wind of doctrine"; after all, he is to help all the church to "grow up" into Christ in all things (Ephesians 4:14, 15).

Surely there are ways in which a congregation can test a man to determine his degree of Christian maturity. There is the diaconate in which he may have served. There are other significant posts in which unordained men may serve with distinction. Above all, the congregation should seek the Lord's face in this matter, earnestly resolving to be guided by his Word. The Holy Spirit will lead a congregation to a safe determination as to when a gifted man is ready for being ordained.

The burden of proof is nevertheless against "taking a chance." "Necessity as the mother of invention" has no application here. To "see" in a man that which the Lord has not given him is gross folly. The wiser course is "better to be safe than sorry" when choosing men to be elders.

A bishop must have a good report

"Moreover he must have *a good report of them that are without.*" At first sight this seems strange. What does the outside world know about Christian maturity and spiritual gifts? Did Jesus not say, "Blessed are ye when men shall revile you . . . for my sake" (Matthew 5:11)?

But the world is not altogether stupid. Worldly people recognize an honest man when they see one. They soon discover, in the course of their everyday affairs, who is to be trusted. They may take delight in the untrustworthiness of one who "has gone kooky on religion," but when such a man stands out as a man of his word they will know it.

So, Peter writes concerning the man who is always ready to give an answer for his Christian hope, that he must have "a good conscience; that, whereas they speak evil of you, as evildoers, they may be ashamed that falsely accuse your good conversation [manner of life] in Christ" (1 Peter 3:16). Again, in the words of Paul, speaking for himself and those with him, he says that they have "renounced the hidden things of dishonesty, not walking in craftiness, . . . but by manifestation of the truth commending ourselves to every man's conscience in the sight of God." (2 Corinthians 4:2).

The urgency of being cautious

We come now to Paul's reasons for urging caution in the choice of elders. The danger is that, "lest being lifted up with pride he fall into the condemnation of the devil"; and "lest he fall into reproach and the snare of the devil" (1 Timothy 3:6, 7).

The church, by exercising its choice of elders ill-advisedly, opens a door for the devil to enter into the affairs of the church and to throw it into turmoil. When this happens the Adversary always wins and the church loses. Satan has a vested interest in "getting to" those who occupy places of service for Christ. Those in high office have farther to fall. David in his adultery and murder, and Peter in his denial of the Lord, are both cardinal examples.

But the church, through hasty action, may even be throwing the man himself into the devil's snare. A man, young in the faith, unaware of the virulent power and corruption that still assails the life of the Christian, may be wide open to the temptation to pride. And pride is the mother sin. God hates it; the devil loves it. "Pride goeth before destruction, and a haughty spirit before a fall" (Proverbs 16:18).

Then, when the novice falls (as he well may do when elevated to an eminence for which he is unprepared), guess who will be there to accuse him and tell him that he is not even a child of God, that God will never forgive such a sinner as he is? The devil, given access to a believer's thought through a lack of vigilance, will influence the thoughts of a man. He will lead him on to haughtiness and self-justification of his pride and so blow him up even higher. Then, when the inevitable crash comes, the father of lies will suddenly switch tactics, from promoting thoughts of self-justification to those of self-condemnation. So convincing can he be to the fallen novice that the poor man will not even be able to lay hold of the covenant promise of forgiveness (1 John 1:9). The consequences can be devastating; the victim may never fully recover in this life. Ours is a clever and vicious enemy!

The danger of reproach before the world

An unwise choice of a man as an elder can also inflict great damage outside the church. The ordaining of unfit men, especially when their unfitness is in the area of their public morality in all its aspects, is another opened door to the enemy of all righteousness. The presumptuously chosen man may be brought "into reproach and the snare of the devil," and this reproach is that of the outside world.

The world outside the church is already in the devil's power; he is the prince of this world. Satan is the spirit that now works in the children of disobedience (Ephesians 2:2). It is easy for him to magnify the instabilities, the weaknesses, and the foibles of the Christian, the best of whom are far from perfect! This is a problem for every believer.

But when the church elevates a man to the highest office (under Christ) in Christ's church, it says in effect, "Behold one who is like unto Christ, whom we have chosen to teach us about Christ and to bear rule over us in Christ's name." Then that man had better be above reproach in matters of personal godliness and common morality. If the name of Christ is blasphemed before the world because of the church's ill-advised choice, who will be drawn into the services of worship to hear the proclamation of the Word of God?

The danger of a snare for the man

But what does Paul mean by suggesting that the unworthy elder himself will fall into the snare of the devil? This man, whose life will not stand the scrutiny of the world, has a false notion of what personal godliness is and of the need for it as it relates to his own daily walk. And his fellow believers have confirmed him in his folly. He is a man entrapped; his conscience is hardened against any pricking; he is a stranger to self-examination.

Assuming that he is, nevertheless, a true believer, it would be too much to label him a *hypocrite*. Yet such a man harbors hypocrisy in his own bosom. The fact that he is blind to his own inconsistency of life only makes the matter worse. What will it take to open his eyes? Not a constant prayer life, for he has none. Not the admonition of his fellow believers, because he will answer thus: "I'm good enough to have been chosen an elder of the church; who are you to question my personal life?" A situation like this is enough to make the angels weep and the devil to laugh with glee.

Now we can readily see why Paul saved these two qualifications until the end of the list. They apply to and are the explication of the preceding qualifications. The first of these two rules—Let him not be a novice!—relates to a man's judgment of his own gifts and graces. The second—Let him be above reproach!—relates to the man's apprehension (or misapprehension) of the vital importance of public morality and godliness before men.

Both the existence of evil and even the appearance of it are to be shunned by every true man of God. The devil knows how to twist our weaknesses and to exploit our sins to his own ends. He is always on the job; he never takes a vacation. Satan knows what to look for in Christians to cast them down into self-condemnation and to do great harm to the cause of Christ in the process. The devil has innumerable helpers in the demon host, and many among the human race that delight to find excuses to blaspheme their Creator.

Christians are always opening doors for the devil to enter. It's bad enough that the lowly believer is often ensnared. But what is manifestly worse is that the best of churches often give Satan an open invitation to entrap those in the highest office of the church. "How are the mighty fallen, and the weapons of war perished! (2 Samuel 1:27).

8

SEEKING THE OFFICE AND THE MAN

At this point, I am beginning a new phase in dealing with the subject of the elders in Christ's church. I have tried to set down the biblical principles governing the eldership. These were summarized at the beginning of this study. And what was found to be biblical is now taken as normative for what is to follow.

This phase is intended to give guidelines to churches, sessions or consistories, prospective and existing elders, to show how these high principles may be put into practice to the edification of the churches. These principles are not for framing to the admiration of passers-by. They are for living. And these grand principles our sovereign God has given for the government of his church are to be practiced in the life of that church.

These are the practical areas I intend to deal with in this and later articles: (1) *Seeking the office and the man;* (2) *Screening procedures;* (3) *Between election and ordination;* (4) *Toward functioning elders;* and (5) *Divisions of labor within the one office.*

Finding the right men

Finding qualified rulers for the church has always been a difficult and serious business. Even the apostle Paul did not immediately ordain elders in the churches he established during his first missionary journey. Instead, he returned sometime later for the purpose of confirming the brethren and then ordaining elders in every church (Acts 14:21-23). Time and care were needed, even under apostolic rule.

How frequently new congregations are organized today before qualified men are found to bear rule in Christ's name. The results are sad — either unfit men chosen in haste, or outside rulers assigned to oversee the congregation without being able to live and worship among those they are to rule. Both expedients are just that — expedients. And the church of Christ suffers.

Yet there still stands this statement of simple fact upon which the church can rest in confidence: "And he [the ascended Lord] gave . . . some, pastors and teachers" (Ephesians 4:11). Our Savior is still the giving Lord who continues to supply his church with pastor-teachers. We can depend upon him.

But it isn't as though these gifted men were dropped down into the lap of the church like bundles from heaven, fully prepared for their labors. Rather, in confident obedience the church must take up two lines of action that, under the blessing of God's Spirit, will result in this promised supply of God's men for God's work. Men must be encouraged to seek the office, and the church must be taught to seek the men of God's appointment.

Seeking the office

Paul writes, "This is a true saying, If a man desire the office of a bishop [elder], he desires a good work" (1 Timothy 3:1). That Paul calls this a true saying, or "faithful word," indicates that it was to be axiomatic in the church, a proposition beyond the need of proof or defense. And what is the proposition? It is that desiring the office of elder is both commendable on the part of the man and good for the church of Christ.

We have little difficulty with this saying as it applies to that aspect of the eldership we call the gospel ministry. Young men whose hearts burn to serve their Redeemer, men who appear to have the gifts, are encouraged to consider the ministry and often are substantially aided in their formal preparation for it. But strangely, it is different when we come to the aspect of this same office that we call the ruling eldership. It is tacitly assumed that any man who *wants* to be an elder is suspect from the start. In fact, if he really wants to serve, he'd be well advised to "play hard

43

to get"!

This is all wrong! Scripture says that to desire the office is to desire to serve the Lord in a good work. Of course, wrong motivation is to be avoided. But when a man desires out of a pure heart to serve his Lord in this high office, the sooner he begins to think about it the better.

Every Christian man may well be encouraged to soliloquize after this fashion: *I have been bought with the precious blood of Christ; therefore, I am not my own. Since I have but one life to live for my Lord and Savior, I must invest it where it will bring him the highest return. And where is the highest place of usefulness in the cause of Christ's kingdom? Is it not in service as one of Christ's undershepherds? I shall pray and prepare myself for this office if it shall please him to confirm his gifts in me. And when he calls me through the call of his church, I will follow him.*

To be sure, a man must examine his gifts. He may need to conclude on good grounds that he is not gifted to fulfill this high calling. But if he desires the office out of a heart burning with zeal and gratitude, woe to that pastor or adult Christian counsellor who may quench his zeal! In fact, the teaching ministry of the church would do well to encourage young men to think in these terms.

Young Christian men, on their part, ought to confide their thoughts to their elders so that the latter may encourage and instruct them in their early preparations for the office. Young men need guidance in the matters of lively devotional habits and solid Bible studies. They need to be given scope within the church to use and develop their gifts. Having proved themselves in small matters, they should be given larger responsibilities. In other words, preparation for the eldership ought to begin long before a man is nominated to stand for election. It is thus that the Holy Spirit makes men bishops.

Seeking the man

Men ought to seek the office. But men must also be sought out for the office. Churches that stand in need of elders are not reluctant to do this. It seems to be quite natural to look around to see who might be available.

But churches are not always wise in the *way* they seek

44

for men. Often the church settles for the best man available. Frequently they look toward men of means and prestige, supposing that if such men are made elders they will use their means and prestige to the advancement of the church. Or the members of the congregation, considering themselves unqualified to make significant choices, will simply rubber-stamp the selections of their session or official nominating committee. All these ways are wrong.

In selecting the seven men for service, the early church was told: "Look ye out among you seven men of honest report, full of the Holy Ghost and wisdom, whom we may appoint over this business" (Acts 6:3). Apparently the members of the congregation were perfectly able to judge who had a good name in the community, who was full of the Spirit, who had genuine wisdom. And the apostles were satisfied with the church's choice. (The number seven was apparently the number needed to do the work. How many men there ought to be on a session is a matter of judging the needs and of finding those qualified to fill them.)

Initiative needs to be taken by those who teach in the church to encourage men to seek the office. But the teaching ministry also needs to instruct congregations in the exercise of discrimination in their search for candidates. Then the church ought to seek and find those (*all* those and *only* those) whom the Lord, through the ministry of the Spirit, has equipped to serve in that particular congregation. This alone should determine the size of a given session. An alert congregation, properly instructed in the relevant Scriptures, will watch its young men as they mature, will pray for the Spirit's wisdom, will plead with the Head of the church to send them pastor-teachers. Then when such men appear and are ready, the congregation should choose them and put them into possession of the office.

Seeking, for the Lord's blessing

It is my firm belief that, if the churches of Christ that desire to be led of the Lord in these matters will follow through on these two lines of seeking, many of the problems that have deadened or shattered churches would be solved. The lessons from Old Testament Israel should make it clear that the church, when it exercises godly care in the selection of its rulers and teachers, is in the way of blessing, awakening, and revival.

A few questions for discussion are given below. I believe they are worthy of deep pondering in the light of this and prior studies of this high office of elder in Christ's church.

1. In the light of the principles we have seen and the discussion so far, which is more scriptural — term eldership (usually a three-year term) or life tenure? What are some of the implications to be drawn from the oneness of the office of minister and ruling elder for this question of the length of time an elder should serve?

2. If men are to be publicly encouraged to desire the office of the elder, how are we to avoid causing that man to feel hurt if the church rejects him?

3. Term eldership is argued as a good means for avoiding (a) having to live for endless years with a bad choice, and (b) establishing a perpetual ruling clique in a congregation. Does term eldership really accomplish these goals? Is life tenure hopelessly subject to these dangers?

4. If the ultimate in usefulness in Christ's church be judged as that of ministering the gospel, is it therefore a matter of lesser honor and usefulness for a young man to aspire to be "just a ruling elder"? Does 1 Timothy 3 support such an attitude, or have we allowed it to develop from some source other than Scripture?

9

SCREENING PROCEDURES

The Holy Spirit makes men bishops or elders (Acts 20: 28). We must never forget this. Nevertheless, elders do not spring forth before the church, Minerva-like, fully perfected. Gifts for teaching and rule must be there, but these need to be developed. Along with that must also come the maturing and seasoning work of biblical sanctification. And this work of sanctification must have progressed to a considerable degree before a man is ordained.

In the last section, I sought to show how men ought to seek the office of elder, and how the leaders of the church ought to encourage promising men to prepare themselves to that end. In this installment, I want to counsel the church in the technique of observing, of recognizing the maturing process in gifted men, in order to choose that man Christ has given to his church.

Waiting for the Lord's provision

Just here churches need to be cautioned against haste in electing men on the basis of *supposed need*. It is dangerous enough for a church's spiritual health to assume it has all the elders it "needs." But the danger of laying hands suddenly on a man just to fill the required number is the greater danger to most congregations. Just because the number of ruling elders has been reduced to near the zero point is no excuse for suddenly saying, "We've got to get some new elders right away!"

The sovereign Lord is fully aware of our needs. He will, if his people wait on him, raise up *his* men in *his* time.

Too often the church acts in the manner of King Saul, who arrogated to himself the prerogatives of God's priest when Samuel failed to show up at the appointed time (1 Samuel 13:5-14). *It is far better to delay organizing a new congregation, or adding to an established session, until the Lord's time has come and his men have been made ready.*

But how do we discern the Lord's time and the Lord's men? It is not by "reading" the congregation to determine if the church has reached a certain level of need. Like the godly woman who concludes that the Lord doesn't want her to be married yet since no suitable man has asked her, the church may need to conclude that the Lord doesn't intend for it to have any new elders just now.

God's way is rather that the church "look out among you . . . men of honest report, full of the Holy Ghost and of wisdom" (Acts 6:3), possessing the qualifications set forth in 1 Timothy 3:2-7 and Titus 1:6-9. This attitude of alert observation and searching must be taught to a congregation — it doesn't come naturally. And it must be put into practice continually, not merely at certain times.

Every adult male member of the congregation should be under scrutiny. Not only ought members ask themselves, "Is this man Spirit-filled, Spirit-gifted, and therefore to be made an elder?" but also, "Given time to mature and develop his gifts, should this man be made an elder in years to come?"

Check-list for screening

At this point some sort of check-list should be drawn up and used by members of the congregation. This is not to "keep score" on these men for a permanent record. But members can and should check men out, privately, according to some such list as this:

Family life: 1. Does he rule his children with firmness and love, or are they inclined to be wild and "bratty"? 2. Does he have a good relationship with his wife, ruling her *and* cherishing her according to the standard of Ephesians 5:25-28? Is his marriage a model to young people in the church? 3. Is their home hospitable, open to the saints in need of fellowship and sustenance; is it a "home away from home" to strangers?

Church life: 1. Are he and his family faithful to *all* the regular services of the church, and not on-again-off-again participants? 2. Is he friendly and cordial toward members and visitors? Does he show concern for the sick, the burdened, the children, the elderly? 3. Does he give of himself in money, time and talents to the Lord's work in the church? Is he willing to take on jobs in the church, without seeking acclaim? 4. Is he firm and decisive in his attitudes about essentials of faith and living without being opinionated or contentious about details? Can he take correction gracefully when he is wrong? Is he able to disagree, without being disagreeable, and willing to see another's point of view? 5. Above all, is he a man of the Word and prayer? Is he eager to learn, able to discern spiritual things, walking close to his Lord? Does he make himself available to those with burdens, listening to their cries, comforting them in sorrows, praying with and for them in their needs? Does he keep confidences? Can he communicate the truth to others and defend it against attack? Is he slow to judge others, quick to commend, and firm in rejecting all forms of gossip?

Worldly affairs: 1. Is he scrupulously honest in all his money matters, giving value for value, paying his debts promptly? 2. Is he respected by those most closely associated with him in day to-day employment? 3. Is he prudent in the use of his worldly wealth, neither slovenly nor showy, and not inordinately attached to his earthly possessions? 4. Does he respond as a Christian should to disappointment and worldly reverses (1 Cor. 7:29-31; Job 1:21, 2:10)?

Finding the Lord's choice

These questions cover the list of qualifications given in 1 Timothy and Titus. It will not be easy to make right judgments in every case, but the church is obliged to work at it anyway. Surely if the whole congregation is prayerfully and quietly on the watch for men such as this, certain things will follow.

It will become apparent quite early that some men are ungifted and unfitted. Very early also a few, or perhaps only one, will begin to stand out from the rest. Certain young men in the church, not noticed before, will now be seen as God's men in the making. Those presently qualified will appear so to all.

In fact, if ten ordinary members of any congregation would follow these principles prayerfully and consistently for one year, and only then share their thinking about which men are truly qualified, the measure of agreement might astound them. God *does* lead his people, often even in spite of their lack of concern to be led. But when his people seek his leading through the diligent use of appointed means, their belief in the Lord's present leadership of his church is marvelously confirmed to the delight of his people and the praise of his name.

These procedures should be followed by all adult voting members of the congregation. At the same time, the existing elders should take the lead in selecting and proposing men for office. But if the whole church, with prayer for the Lord's guidance, has followed this procedure of seeking the Lord's men, there will be no rebellion or resentment in the ranks because this man or that is passed by. The reasons for passing him by will be apparent to all, and thus the people will have closed a door to the devil who often uses this situation to divide and destroy a congregation of Jesus Christ.

Practical means for spiritual ends

The rest is simple enough. It is a good thing to have safeguards (in the church's by-laws) against hasty and injudicious nominations. These will not do the job alone, and lack of them is not fatal if the church has been doing its homework. Naturally, no name ought to be proposed for election (either by the session or members of the congregation) unless it can be published at least one month prior to election; even three or six months' advance notice is preferable. Nor should a name be published without the nominee's own carefully considered consent.

And it should not be made more difficult for ordinary members to propose names than for the session. After all, it is the people themselves who must submit to the rule of those elders they elect. In any case, a nominee ought to be warned that nomination is not tantamount to election; his prayer should be that the Lord will provide the best for his church.

Another caution: Ordinarily a man would be wise not to accept election if a significant minority is opposed to him. Unless it is clear that he was opposed for improper motives, he should decline the office. Otherwise, he places upon the dissidents the difficult task of rendering submission in the Lord to a man they feel is unqualified to rule in the Lord's name. This would jeopardize his ministry to them from the very outset.

Then there is the matter of competition for office, as when there are more nominees that there are offices to be filled. This is an inherent danger where sessions are organized with term-eldership and a fixed number of places to be filled in each class. To set a fixed number of elders is a dangerous precedent. True, there were twelve apostles and seven deacons; but these numbers were determined by the Lord himself. It is far better for us to seek the men of God's own choosing, however many or few there may be, and to make them elders. To fill the posts with unqualified men or to refuse those who are qualified just because we have "enough" already is to refuse the Lord's own provisions for his church.

We should be extremely cautious in choosing elders lest we tempt some men to run whom the Lord never sent (Jeremiah 23:21)! But if a man is ready to serve Christ's church as an elder, by what arbitrary rule is he to be kept back because another man is also ready? If the Holy Spirit makes men elders, then the church ought to be ruled by those men the Spirit has prepared. (But if a church insists on choosing *between* candidates, then the man chosen by majority should be voted on again to determine if the minority is prepared to submit to his rule in the church.)

The Holy Spirit makes men bishops. He makes bishops of those whom he first makes men. He makes men bishops by giving them gifts for teaching and rule. He makes men ready for this service by maturing them in their gifts and by the work of sanctification in their lives. Chronological age is not the primary rule; but we do need to beware of making *bishops* of men whom the Lord has not yet made *elders* in wisdom, discernment, and spiritual graces. To ordain a novice is only to minister confusion to the flock of Christ.

Questions to ponder:

1. If a man ardently desires and seeks the office of elder, but is rejected by the church, what counsel should be given to help him accept the failure of his cherished desire?

2. May a man's success in business or profession be a partial measure of his suitability for the office of elder? In what ways?

3. Should a church choose elders during a time of dissension and turmoil in the congregation?

4. What are the mechanics best suited for a congregation to arrive at consensus on the candidates proposed? How openly should a man's qualifications be discussed before taking a vote? Is there any way to prevent this process of discerning who has the qualifications from becoming a matter of common gossip?

10

BETWEEN ELECTION AND ORDINATION

In this third part of our discussion of the application of principles, we come to consider what can be done between the election and ordination of new elders. I have already tried to show how there is an interaction between potential elders and congregations seeking elders.

The man seeks the office out of holy motives; the congregation seeks the man whom God has prepared to teach and rule in the name, and by the authority of Christ. Thus both potential candidates and congregations are in position to be led by the Holy Spirit. And they can depend on him to do just that. In a word, we all need to become familiar with the workings of the sovereign Spirit, that we neither run ahead of nor lag behind him, but follow with him wherever he leads.

Let me repeat that in so doing a local congregation may see fit to hedge the power of members to nominate men of their choice. But it should not be made overly difficult for them to nominate those whom they believe are "of honest report, full of the Holy Ghost and of wisdom" (Acts 6:3). It is in the congregation's interest to exercise a full and free choice since it is they who must yield submission to these same men in the Lord.

A training period

Once the choice is made, *is it just a matter of course to ordain and install?* This is an important question. I confess that we have no explicit commandment in Scripture on this; nevertheless there are strong biblical suggestions. Jesus chose twelve disciples to be with him (Mark 3:13, 14). These twelve continued with him for up to three years before they were commissioned as apostles (John 20:21-23). To be an apostle required one to have been present for quite some time with Jesus during his earthly ministry (Acts 1:21, 22).

Again, Saul of Tarsus, though he met the Lord himself on the road to Damascus, spent three years much of which was in solitary preparation for his later work. Even after his sojourn in Arabia, Saul did not immediately launch into his life's calling but was in Tarsus and Antioch for at least a year before the Holy Spirit sent him forth to the Lord's work (see Galatians 1:14-17; Acts 11:25, 26; 13:1-3).

Even in the case of these infallibly called men there was need for preparation and seasoning before they were put into full possession of their ministry. How much more when the choice of men rests upon fallible human judgment!

Now these cautions are seriously observed in the choosing and ordaining of those elders commonly known as ministers of the gospel. These men are normally expected to earn a college degree and complete a three-year theological course before they are eligible to consider a call to the office of pastor, evangelist, or teacher. Whatever we may think of the need for this kind of preparation, there is at least a correlation between the training of ministers and that given to the original apostles.

But beyond this case the correlation between biblical model and contemporary practice ends. In some Reformed churches men are elected and almost immediately installed. The standards of the Orthodox Presbyterian Church do not require even so much as a formal examination of elders-elect before they are ordained. Nor is there any requirement that ruling elders be ordained by the laying on of hands, even though this is done in most congregations.

I cannot accept as biblical what many American Presbyterians hold—that the office of ruling elder is essentially different from that of the minister of the Word. This is not to say that *all* elders ought normally to be holders of college and seminary degrees. (In a later article I hope to show that, while the function of all elders is one of teaching *and* rule, there is a diversity of functions within the visible church.)

For now, I would plead for more serious consideration of ways and means of giving adequate preparation and testing of elders-elect before they are ordained and installed.

Suggestions for training

I have been preplexed for many years over the wide divergence between the training and testing required of ministers and that of ruling elders. It seems we've come a long way from the simplicity of New Testament practice. This is not to call for any lowering of standards for candidates to the ministry. But I do plead for raising the standards of elder-competence to the point where we can at least view the various functions of the one office of elder within a single perspective. In other words, *we ought not so to concentrate on a trained and competent ministry that, by default, we are content to accept an ignorant and untried ruling eldership.*

But how are we to avoid the latter within the existing framework of today's Reformed and Presbyterian churches? Let me suggest the following as an acceptable program:

1. A return to the practice of encouraging and grooming young men for possible leadership, together with training of congregations in the technique of seeking and discerning who are Spirit-filled, Spirit-gifted men, will go a great distance toward readying God's men for service in the church.

Paul instructed Timothy to commit the deposit of truth to faithful men who could teach others also (2 Timothy 2:2). These faithful men would emerge in the manner suggested in the two previous articles. "Faithful men" are born, not made. That is, men may be born into the kingdom with potential gifts, but these need developing. It may be years before a quite gifted man has gained the maturity for ruling in the church.

It is also most important that churches recognize gifted men; at the same time, churches must know when a man is really ready to begin the exercise of his gifts in the highest offical capacity. Both a discernment of gifts and a clear view of when they are ready for use is required, and an error in judgment may well be disastrous.

Testing the elder-elect

2. What is said above applied to the time *before* a man is

elected to office. But even that is not enough in itself. No amount of formal training will make an elder out of an ungifted man; nevertheless, gifted men do need a certain amount of formal training.

As a minimum, elders need to know the doctrines of Scripture, Reformed doctrine, both systematically and exegetically. That is, they must have a grasp of the "theological catalog" of truth so that each vital doctrine is understood in its relation to the whole. This means an elder ought to be master of the Shorter Catechism and fully at home in the Larger Catechism and the Confession of Faith (or other similar Reformed standards).

But the elder must also know how the grand truths of our standards arise out of the Word of God. It is not sufficient that he merely agree with these secondary standards of the church; he also needs to see that the system of truths set forth in them is in fact a correct expression of what is taught in Scripture. This is high idealism! But who can honestly and solemnly take the ordination vows upon any lesser conviction?

Similarly, the elder should have a solid grasp and warm consent to the form of presbyterial government and discipline of the church which he is to serve as an ordained ruler.

3. A man needs some training in ministering the Word both to individual believers and to the unsaved upon whom he must lay the claims of Christ. I believe there is need for a manual specially designed for this purpose. If elders are co-shepherds with the principal minister of the Word, they ought to be taught some of the basic rules for shepherding Christ's sheep—before they learn bad ones in this crucial part of their service. We all know that bad habits are more easily not learned than unlearned!

It is also during this period between election and ordination that existing sessions should undertake the instruction of elders-elect in the formal knowledge suggested above. In cases where acting elders failed to receive such training themselves, special efforts are in order to remedy the deficiency. Then if, in the process of this training, some man should be honestly convinced that he has grave deficiencies in the gifts required or in competence and acceptance of the church's doctrines and government, he would not be acting sinfully if he were to relinquish the office. Especially is this so if the man is convinced that such skill and competence are beyond his reach.

Passing an examination

4. There is one more step to take before ordination, if only to be assured that the first three have been successfully surmounted. Elders-elect should be tested as to their knowledge of Scripture doctrine, the church's government, and of their ability to use the sword of the Spirit in the battles of the Lord.

It has long been my practice to require every newly elected elder to undergo trials before the session prior to ordination. It is no injustice to a man, if need be, to have him wait some months to complete his instruction and examination. These men should be given the privilege of sitting in on session meetings during this time of preparation, both as part of the training and a preview of what is to come.

But this matter of testing should be taken seriously and not treated as a mere token. Nor should it be viewed as either tragic or unjust if a man is honestly judged to be unqualified for office even after being elected by the congregation. Whom do we aim to please in all this, the man himself, the members of the congregation, or the King and Head of the church?

When one of God's choice men has been in training in the school of Christ from the hour of his spiritual birth; after he has lived an exemplary life for many years in one or more praying, discerning congregations; when he has completed a rigorous training in the use of God's Word in all sorts of life situations; and when he has successfully undergone thorough questioning of his knowledge of the doctrines and government of Christ's church—after all this, what a day of joy, for him and for the people, when he kneels before God in front of the congregation and is solemnly set apart for the holy office of undershepherd for Jesus Christ! That day might well be counted the greatest day since he had been born anew, a day for rejoicing by all good men and angels.

Questions for pondering:

1. Our Lord knew that Judas would never qualify as one of the apostles. Yet he chose him to be among the twelve. Why did the Lord do this? What does it suggest concerning the subjects discussed in this article?

2. What has happened in the last nineteen hundred years to put such a large difference between the training and qualifications required for ministers and those expected of ruling elders? Has this difference resulted in downgrading the ruling elder, upgrading the office of the minister?

3. Does the increase in the variety of versions and paraphrases of Scripture make it more important for elders to be clear discerners of the Word? Why?

4. Under what circumstances would an existing elder, though he continues to live a blameless life, be well advised to relinquish his office? In what circumstances might his experience as an elder serve to counteract any shortage of gifts such a man might have?

11

FUNCTIONING IN THE OFFICE

We commonly think of a distinction between active and inactive elders: an *active* elder is serving as a member of a session; an *inactive* elder is one not serving on a session. Yet I have known elders not on any session who are very active elders indeed, and I have known many session members who are quite inactive.

The "inactive" session member

I do not wish to make a case for technically calling non-session members "active elders." In fact, I do not believe that any man whom the Holy Spirit has made a bishop (elder) has any right to *be* inactive by his own choice. He may be a true elder and become inactive by reason of age or infirmity. But that cannot be regarded as a matter of his own choice!

Or an elder may find it necessary to move from one congregation to another. In such a case he must wait on the Lord for the new congregation to see in him the gifts of office and thrust him once more into the active eldership in this new congregation. But waiting for God's people to choose him cannot be construed as a matter of willful inactivity either.

But the tragedy of inactivity is seen when a man with proven gifts, with the call of God and the concurrence of a congregation of Christ, is placed on the session, yet fails to use his gifts in the service of the Head of the church. Were I in this man's place, I would be conscious of standing in jeopardy of the Lord when he said, "No man, having put his hand to the plough, and looking back, is fit for the kingdom of heaven" (Luke 9:62). Paul, whom Christ called to the apostolic office, said, "Woe is unto me if I preach not the gospel" (1 Corinthians 9:16).

So let the man called and confirmed in the office of elder likewise say, "Woe is unto me if I do not shepherd Christ's flock." There is no place in Christ's church for a non-functioning elder if he has it within him to do the work of the elder, nothing hindering him. These are strong words that I shall attempt to justify in what follows.

The undershepherd's labor

First, let us review what the elder's work is. It is the work of teaching and rule as an undershepherd of Christ—not rule alone or teaching alone, but both in integration and balance. If an elder sits on session and does no more than that part of his task, he is not a fully functioning elder. Such an elder cannot possibly have the "feel" for the flock over which he is supposed to rule.

We have an excellent insight into this from Acts 6:4. The apostles had their hands full in dealing with the problems of the church at that time. Then came the complaint from certain widows alleging neglect in material ministrations. The complaint appeared to be just. But what should the apostles do? What they did was to choose seven men to serve ("be deacons") in this ministration, "but we (the apostles) will give ourselves continually to prayer, and to the ministry of the word." These apostles were elders extraordinary. If they must be primarily engaged in prayer and the Word, how much more should this be so of the permanent rulers in the church?

So too in Hebrews 13:17 where the believers were admonished to obey those who had the rule over them. And the reason for this submission is that the elders "watch for your souls, as they that must give account." To watch over the souls of men, being accountable to the chief Shepherd (1 Peter 5:4), is a solemn and arduous labor.

When Paul says (1 Timothy 5:17) to give "double honor" to those who rule well, "especially they who labour in the word and doctrine (teaching)," he is *not* excluding teaching from the work of ruling. It is not that some elders rule while others also teach. But already in 1 Timothy 3:2, 4, Paul has combined aptness to teach and rule as the duties of an elder.

We are therefore to interpret the words "labour in the word and doctrine" with the emphasis on *labour*. Some elders, among those who rule well, are called to give themselves so fully to the office of teaching that they are especially to receive that support necessary for them to be "free from worldly care and avocations." But "word and doctrine" are tied to the need to "rule well" as complementary parts of the official work of the elder.

We can summarize *the function of the elder's office* as a deep involvement for the flock of Christ, calling for *much watching and prayer, wherein every elder is accountable to the chief Shepherd for the feeding, leading, and disciplining of the souls committed to his care.*

It remains for the next (and last) article in this series to detail more fully the division of labor within the office. Just now, it seems wise to list some of the specific functions in which all elders need to be actively engaged. It goes without saying that the degree of involvement may vary widely. This is implied in 1 Timothy 5:17. Still, *every* elder, it seems to me, needs to be engaged in every one of these three basic functions of office:

1. Teaching

This stands at the head of the list. I do not advocate that ruling elders ought to take to the pulpit at the first opportunity. Those with gifts for the public proclamation of the Word should do this on appropriate occasions. But most elders are not so gifted, and so have no call to official preaching of the Word.

Apart from official preaching in the pulpit, all elders can be and ought to be involved in the pastor's ministry of the Word. The elders are to listen, sitting before the preacher in the same position as the rest of the flock. They are to pray that the Word from his lips may have free course and be glorified with the Spirit's blessing, advising the pastor both positively and negatively—always constructively—with that end in view.

Then too, the elders need to be often in the homes of the congregation, exhorting on the basis of that same preached Word and directly admonishing from the Word as needed. Add to this the opportunities an elder has to minister the Word of life to those outside, confuting the gainsayers both within and without. It should be easily apparent that the ministry of every elder is, to a very significant extent, a teaching ministry.

2. Praying

Prayer is also primary to the elder's calling. Every believer ought to care for the souls of his fellow believers, but elders have it committed unto them by the Lord himself to watch for men's souls. This responsibility must not lie lightly on his conscience. But he needs to go many times to a brother or sister, unbidden, to warn of sin and the danger of falling into sin. Does he dare undertake such a solemn task without first having wrestled in prayer for that brother or sister? Apart from prayer, where will he get that authority which is recognizable in a true man of God?

Indeed, how are the members of the flock—especially the lambs—to know their elders as men who love them in Christ, unless they can discern in the elder's voice and demeanor that he truly loves them? Here is the secret of functioning eldership—elders who are preeminently men of prayer. And I should add that elders need to pray together, especially to pray with their pastor for the seal of God upon his ministry and for the needs of the flock.

3. Ruling

The pinnacle of the elder's labor is that of rule. But I must say that if ruling is looked upon as all, or nearly all, there is to being an elder, then such a man will *not* rule well. In fact, he as yet knows nothing truly about rule in the church of Christ.

The *session* is a *sitting* of the members of a *court of Jesus Christ.* They are judges "in Israel." And the biblical concept of judging includes far more than the judicial function, as in disciplining offenders. It also includes the executive function—wearing a crown for King Jesus! Elders need to grasp this concept which our Presbyterian heritage has passed on to us.

Now the elder who rules for Jesus is also under the rule of Jesus, even as every worthy jurist is a man of the law and, even more than others, a man under the law. Men who sit in the seat of Christ in ruling over the church must know what it means to be "under the law to Christ" (1 Corinthians 9:21). In making decisions, an elder has no liberty to follow his own inclinations, but is bound by the Word of God. So, when matters come before a session of worthy men, involving issues of doctrine or life, these men will be so fully men of the Word that they will speak from God's Word with one voice. True, in administrative matters there will be differences of opinion—though even here unanimity of heart. But in the great subject of the application of the gospel to the life and witness of the church, the elders will be as one before both God and men. Thus will they bear rule in the house of God.

So it comes to this: Functioning elders do indeed function in the highest sense when they sit as courtiers of the King of kings—whether on sessional, presbyterial, or synodical levels. This is indeed the pinnacle of their labors. Yet they do not begin their labors in session. They begin them over the open Bible in earnest study; on their knees praying for the saints; among their people laboring, exhorting, encouraging, comforting, ministering to the flock over whom God has made them bishops. Only from there are they ready to move up to sit in the seat of Christ to judge the flock according to the Word of Christ that lives and abides forever.

Questions for pondering:

1. If we accept the premise that an elder may not voluntarily cease to function as an elder, what justification can we advance for the common, American practice of term eldership?

2. Does not the demanding nature of the elder's function, as advanced in this article, throw a strain on those gifted men called to serve even while they must follow such other demanding professions as that of medicine or law?

3. Are we not in danger of frightening off some potentially useful servants of Christ when we so strongly emphasize the demands of the eldership on a man?

4. What are the best ways for elders to share the prayer burden with their pastor? Meeting with him just before the worship service? on Saturday evenings? What other answers would you suggest?

12

THE DIVISION OF LABOR

In this concluding article, I want to lay stress on the fact that the Spirit's qualifying gifts are given to different men in differing measure. While it is fundamental to understand that all God-appointed elders need to be "apt to teach" and able to rule well, and that each is obliged to exercise himself in both of these areas to some degree, nevertheless *they will not all exercise themselves according to an equal measure.*

Our Lord called Paul to be an apostle to the Gentiles, while Peter was to go to the "Circumcision." Even among the original twelve, the disciples were far from equal in gifts or ability to use them. Paul (in 1 Timothy 5:17) implies as much when he says, "Let the elders that rule well be counted worthy of double honor, especially they who labor in word and doctrine."

While it is sad that even then some did not rule well, it is not surprising that some who did rule well labored in the word and doctrine whereas others did not. That is, some devoted themselves more extensively to the Word than did others. Though this passage furnishes some ground for the present-day distinction between the "teaching elder" and the "ruling elder," I doubt that the distinction was that "cut and dried" in Paul's mind or in the practice of the early church. Rather, there seems to be a widely different degree of involvement between certain elders and others in their ministry. The present article seeks to translate this into reasonable principles for action.

Diversity in labor

In today's Reformed churches, the diversity of labor within the eldership is not hard to find. Even among ministers, some labor harder and longer than others (without suggesting reproach to those who labor less). Some ruling elders have more time to give to their respective ministries than do others.

As I have already remarked, no man ought to be put into the office who cannot or will not give a considerable portion both of time and strength to the eldership. Even so, it is a fact that some most worthy men have, in God's providence, less free time and strength away from their wordly toils than is true for others. Some have greater family responsibilities (which they must not neglect!). Some have a stronger physique than others. And some men reach retirement with many years of vigor and good health to make available for the work of Christ in his church.

What can be said for a healthy diversity of labor within this highest continuing office in Christ's church? First, at the risk of being redundant, I will stress again those duties that fall upon all elders; second, I would list certain tasks that elders may follow by way of semi-specialization.

Common tasks for all elders

All elders must be active in each of these areas: 1. They must all minister the Word to, and pray with, the members of the church individually. And here, since I have not done so before, let me commend the practice of "zone" oversight.

In former generations, our Presbyterian forefathers practiced the division of the parish into equal geographical areas, giving one elder responsibility in each such zone. Not having "parishes" in the older sense, our zones must be more arbitrarily determined without reference to the location of a family as the primary factor.

In any case, dividing the whole congregation into "zones" assures an element of oversight to every elder. In some churches a two-man team might be assigned one zone. Or the pastor himself may conduct annual visitation of the families, taking with him the elder assigned to the particular home he is visiting. This is a good method for "breaking in" men new to this sort of thing. But it should not become the normal practice because the elder will tend to be a "silent partner" in the presence of the minister.

I hasten to add that all such devices are only devices. They have their drawbacks. Some families would prefer one elder above another—which could result in certain elders having no families to supervise if such choices were honored. Then too, stated visitations sometimes cause families to tense up and so fail to get full benefit from visits. Nevertheless, devices are useful. Without them I doubt if every elder would receive a share in this ministry.

2. All elders must engage in *ongoing Bible study and prayer* for the blessing of God upon the entire flock. Here the pastor needs to commend this activity to his "co-pastors" (elders are co-shepherds in the scriptural sense). Pastors must see to it that their brethren in labor are spiritually growing and living, taking heed to themselves and to the flock (Acts 20:28).

3. All elders need to take time, individually and in session, to discuss and *pray about the concerns of their flock*. While this may be combined with regular session meetings, such an important function can be crowded out unless time is set aside for the purpose and jealously guarded.

High on the priority list for discussion and prayer should be the mutual exchange of counsel between pastor and elders concerning the scope, content and effectiveness of the pastor's pulpit ministry. Of course, such an exchange needs to be basically constructive and positive; elders are never to forget that their pastor's ministry is, in a very real sense, their own even when he stands in the pulpit to proclaim the gospel.

4. It will not hurt to say again that the crown of the labors of the elders of any church is their *sitting as Christ's representatives* in session meetings. Every elder must participate in every meeting of his session unless providentially prevented from doing so.

Areas of specialization

Within the common functions of the office of elder there are some specializations, areas into which an elder may enter who has special gifts and abilities.

1. I would place *teaching* at the head of the list. This is beyond the normal teaching that all elders are obliged to carry out. Some elders are gifted as teachers, proving their gifts to edification in Sunday school classes, in midweek prayer services, or group Bible study.

But I would raise a caution here. It is only natural that some men aspire to teach. Nevertheless, some who aspire may well be without the gifts or experience needed. Let every man prepare himself, praying for the improvement of the gifts he has and for opportunity to use them. But let him wait patiently upon the Lord until his fellow elders judge him ready.

2. Some elders are gifted as *personal counsellors* and sought out by those in the church who are weighed down with problems. This is especially true with those men who show ability in working with young people. In this area too, let those who appear to have the gifts be urged to prepare themselves. The best available preparation in study and prayer is all too little for one who is thrust into a counselling ministry in these days. There are many good aids available, but let them be chosen with careful discrimination.

3. Some men of God have gifts for *organization.* How useful these gifts can be today when our homeland is becoming increasingly a "foreign" mission field! There is urgent need for the church to break through the shell of conventionality and confront a lost world with the gospel.

Branch Sunday schools, chapels, vacation Bible schools, home Bible study groups, are all available means. But the work needs to be carefully done, and organization is necessary. The elder with organizing gifts need not be the pastor or principal teaching elder. But a man with gifts for handling all the details may well prove to be God's "organization man" in his church. By all means a man of God with such gifts should be given scope to use them that everything may be done "decently and in order" (1 Corinthians 14:40).

4. Still others have gifts for *financial stewardship.* Though the deacons need to be concerned to distribute the gifts of God's people appropriately, and though the church treasurer may well be a deacon or not ordained at all, it

does not follow that the eldership is so heavenly an office as to be of no earthly good. An elder with gifts for financial stewardship should be given opportunity to use them.

Such a man can be a great help to the deacons and the treasurer, suggesting more prudent use of the Lord's money, encouraging them to better stewardship and fiscally sound practices. Such a man can also be of real help to the church, fostering and encouraging the biblical teaching that giving is a grace from God (2 Corinthians 8, 9) and not a necessary chore. Here is a spiritual ministry to challenge the best efforts of God's spiritual men!

5. Other specialized ministries deserve mention. An elder with gifts in music may be employed to develop the gifts of the whole flock in the praise of God. A ministry of writing and editing can be valuable in many churches; a newsletter that goes beyond trivia to be a true spiritual organ is a task worthy of any man with the special abilities. Others may have the rare gift of stating biblical truth in the language of the people so that it may be understood and received. In fact, every distinct gift of God should find a place of exercise in the work of the church; if God gave it, God meant it to be used.

6. One more specialty deserves separate treatment. All elders need to be men of prayer, but God does raise up some to be *giants of prayer*. Who does not thrill at the names of men like Robert Murray M'Cheyne, George Muller, or Praying Hyde? True, the Lord has not been pleased to grant many such men to us today. But there is desperate need for special power before the throne of grace.

To be sure, the Spirit is no respecter of persons, and may well give the gift of prayer to anyone. God gave such a ministry to Anna in the temple (Luke 2:36, 37). Yet elders, just because their office indicates that they have advanced in sanctification, should tend to excell in the life of prayer. The times call for men of this kind. May God give us many who know how to lay hold on God beyond that degree which most of us have attained.

A word of warning

I believe that every man of God needs to be warned to beware of the devil's temptation to jealousy about the superior gifts or tasks of another. If one or two men stand out from the rest in any particular gift, let the others rejoice that God has given such gifts to his church. The other comparable danger is the temptation to pride in those with exceptional gifts. The devil delights in finding such an opening (1 Peter 5:8; cf. John 3:22-25; Philippians 1:12-21; 1 Timothy 3:6).

So I bring this series to a close. The articles have been designed to be of special use to those who bear rule in Christ's church and those who seek the eldership. But let no one think these subjects are of no concern to even the least believer. Choosing, ordaining, obeying, and sitting at the feet of God's called men is the job of all the church.

Pray that Christ's Spirit will continue his working in all our churches; that he will call those choice men, making them eager and willing to serve the Head of the church; that such men may be spiritually recognized by the people; that superior grace may be given them to serve their Lord long and well; that they may stand ready with Paul "not only to be bound, but to die for the name of the Lord Jesus" (Acts 21:13).

Questions for Pondering:

1. One man appears to have all the gifts for eldership, but declines the office because of business pressures. Should he be pressed to reconsider and reorder his business affairs, or should his excuse be accepted?

2. What personal qualities are desirable in one who counsels, either in the context of home visitation or in a more specialized way?

3. Should the pastor do all the specialized calling—on the sick or burdened—or should it be shared with the other elders?

4. Do you think a man should be made an elder because he seems to have one of the gifts of specialized service mentioned?

5. Are the standards for eldership set forth in these articles so high that good men will be discouraged from seeking or accepting the office?